BÔ YIN RÂ
(JOSEPH ANTON SCHNEIDERFRANKEN)

THE GATED GARDEN
VOLUME FIFTEEN

THE MYSTERY
OF GOLGOTHA

For more information
about the books of Bô Yin Râ and
titles available in English translation,
visit the Kober Press web site at
www.kober.com.

BÔ YIN RÂ
(JOSEPH ANTON
SCHNEIDERFRANKEN)

THE MYSTERY
OF GOLGOTHA

TRANSLATED FROM THE GERMAN
BY B.A. REICHENBACH

THE
KOBER
PRESS

BERKELEY, CALIFORNIA

For permission to quote or excerpt, write to:
The Kober Press
2534 Chilton Way
Berkeley, CA 94704

Email: koberpress@mindspring.com

This book is a translation from the German of
Das Mysterium von Golgotha, by Bô Yin Râ
(J.A. Schneiderfranken), published in 1922 by
Verlag Magishe Blätter, Leipzig. The copyright to
the German text is held by Kober Verlag, AG, Bern,
Switzerland.

Printed in the United States of America

International Standard Book Number: 978-0-915034-18-5

Typography and composition by Dickie Magidoff

Book cover after a design by Bô Yin Râ

ACKNOWLEDGMENT

For
Eric W. Strauss,
publisher and editor,
without whose tireless commitment
English translations of
THE GATED GARDEN
would not be in print
to offer insights shedding light
on final things.

CONTENTS

INTRODUCTION

IN THE SAME WAY AS MY BOOK *More Light* combines a series of separate discussions, the present work as well consists of a collection of chapters, each to some degree complete within itself. Even so, I wish to see the parts I here combined considered only in relation to each other. By giving the entire book the title of its opening chapter, I seek to underline that all are equally connected to that chapter's content.

I am confident my readers will be able to approach the book with this in mind and that they need no special hint to find the guiding thread that here unites the separate parts into a single, self-explanatory work.

Among all those who seek a spiritual renewal in our day there are unquestionably many who, from childhood on, revered the radiant Master of Nazareth as a teacher of divine authority; many for whom the mystery of Golgotha stood at the center of their faith.

Deeply rooted faith in the Anointed One may even nowadays inspire inner life in some, while others, plagued by doubts, their souls distressed, have long since lost what in their youth had given them both light and firm belief in God.

For all such readers, I believe, this book will help to lift some of the veils that have concealed from them what to their hearts' profoundest longing could bring enduring certitude.

The foremost need is to reveal the timeless Truth that, in the *Son of God* from Nazareth, had formed itself a life that shall send forth the purest radiance of its light into the farthest ages yet to come, notwithstanding that the present age may harbor serious doubts as to that life's reality.

IMAGES OF THE most varied kinds have through the centuries obscured the life of the sublime embodiment of Love, the radiant Master of the Gospels.

Even at the time when he still walked the lands of Palestine there were only very few that clearly comprehended who he truly was; and those whom sacred scripture speaks of as his pupils can hardly be included in that number.

What has come down to us of words that have preserved his teachings displays the colors of the many who used his sayings to bolster their own fantasies.

There is not much that in this day may still be seen as an authentic record of his life.

In spite of that, however, even the fragments of the narratives continue to display the radiance of a Light that truly is "not of this earth," but therefore needed the active mediation of a "Son of Man" in order to impart itself to mortals here on earth.

TRUTH AND legends in the course of time have come to claim their place within the radiance of that Light.

Symbols of profoundest depth have in its glory sought illumination.

Concepts old and new it had to serve as needed in their quest for light, but seldom only was its real essence truly comprehended.

The radiant Master's God-inspired teachings will not, however, shed their light on the profoundest depths for anyone who reads the ancient records as long as the Master himself remains concealed behind the clouding narratives of scripture.

Those who called themselves his servants were in spirit far too removed from him to discern his true identity; and their concern was for the most part not to question the received reports.

It thus could come about that in a later age, which far too confidently trusted mental knowledge, some would even doubt the Master had indeed existed.

BUT THE ONE, of whom the records have preserved the saying, "I am with you always, even to the end of the world," transcended the dimensions not merely of his servants, but equally of his deniers.

Be grateful if your reading of this book will let you recognize his pure, eternal features.

Even if you are not guided by his teachings —or rather by the teachings one has formulated in his name—you will henceforth count among his own, if once you have discerned the truth of who he was—and is.

You then will read the narratives that tell of him with different eyes, and every cause of doubt you may have had shall be dissolved.

If your belief is nourished by the ancient doctrines that have raised cathedrals on his teachings, then will his light—provided you know how to read—illuminate the darkness of their halls; and many a teaching that was a heavy burden on your shoulders, and which you only dared not question, lest you committed sacrilege, will then become a precious weight to bear, a jewel you will never want to be without.

THE SOURCE to which I owe the knowledge that I here convey to you, the present book will tell you; and here you will indeed be offered insights based on truth and far removed from error and illusion.

I do not want to make you doubt your faith, and I profoundly venerate the altar's sacred vessels; my purpose rather is to give your faith abiding content; and springs whose waters never cease to flow I once again would open up within you.

Take, then, this book and let its words become a blessing in your life.

If you at first should find some things still new and strange, be not too quick in forming any judgments.

You will have to read these pages more than once before the cluttered shafts of your cognition shall be cleared, so that the living waters of your being's inmost depth can rise at last to reach the light.

Bear in mind that many centuries have thrown their rubble down your well and that no one but you yourself can clear out that debris.

❧

"Fools believe themselves great
when they can overcome others;
the sage makes himself small,
that he may conquer—himself."

CHAPTER ONE

THE MYSTERY OF GOLGOTHA

IN THE DAYS OF CONFUCIUS, THERE lived a wondrous sage in the Middle Kingdom, known by the name of Lao Tzu.

Confucius, the great teacher of the laws that govern happiness in life, heard about Lao Tzu and set out to pay him a visit. Having returned from this journey, Confucius walked about in silence for three days, so that his pupils were greatly astonished.

Tseu Kong, however, finally took heart and asked the teacher why he kept silent for so long.

Confucius then replied and said, "When I notice that a man will use his thoughts to escape me like a bird in flight, I use my own thoughts like arrows one shoots from a bow.

I never fail to hit such a man, and thus become his master.

"If he would elude me like a fleet-footed stag, I pursue him like a skillful hound; I overtake him without fail and throw him to the ground.

"If he tries to evade me like a fish that slips into the deep, I use my fishing rod to catch him, and bring him under my control.

"But a dragon that soars into the sky and rides upon the clouds, I am unable to pursue.

"I have seen Lao Tzu, and he is like that dragon; when he spoke, my mouth stood open and I could not close it. My tongue was hanging from my mouth in sheer amazement and I had no strength to pull it back; my soul, however, was in turmoil, and it has not yet regained its peace."

THESE FEW words, preserved in the writings of China, vividly describe the overwhelming impression which the spiritual wisdom of Lao Tzu had made upon Confucius, who surely also was a sage in his own way, but one who solely mastered the dimension of the intellect, while the former's spiritual home lay far above all intellectual knowledge.

According to tradition, Lao Tzu, having reached old age, near the end of his life, left his country and made his way to the West, toward the land from which he had received his wisdom.

In the *Tao Te Ching*, which is ascribed to him, one may search for the essential content of his teachings.

It has been pointed out, and not without all reason, how closely these teachings resemble those of the Pythagoreans and the philosophy of Plato; indeed, one sought to make it plausible that Lao Tzu had drawn upon the wisdom of ancient Egyptian mysteries; and in this way the strangest of connections were imagined.

As nearly always in similar cases, a grain of truth lies at the bottom of such suppositions; for Lao Tzu, whom the wisest worldly thinker of his age had regarded with such awe, was one of the few publicly active Masters of the spiritual community, symbolically referred to as "The White Lodge," to which not only all the ancient mystery cults, but also Plato and Pythagoras had owed their very best.

But while this spiritual community as such had throughout the millennia been active on this earth exclusively in spiritual ways, and only from complete seclusion, at given times, albeit very seldom, there have been certain of its members who were "living in the world," but found themselves prepared and willing to make public, also through the spoken and the written word, spiritual wisdom of the highest kind; and one of those exceptions was the sage Lao Tzu.

He had good reasons when he stated that the sage needs to consider time and circumstances in his teachings; for he knew very well that what he taught could not be comprehended by people in his day unless it were presented in a form that might gain recognition at least among the spiritually-minded in his age.

Time and circumstances were conditions that each of the exceptional members of "The White Lodge" who was living in the world had always to consider when he sought to put his teachings into words. Nor was the radiant Lord of Love, who called these teachings "joyous news," less mindful of his mission than of the need to take account of time and circumstances, and to attach the guide line of his teachings where it could rely on firm support. Firm support, however, at the same time always will prove firm resistance.

One will not comprehend the all-surpassing greatness of the life, the teachings, and the works of the Anointed, who through his Love became the most exalted among all those who know themselves as *Luminaries of primordial Light*, and as the *Words of the primordial Word*, unless one recognizes that also he was obligated wisely to make use of time and circumstances; indeed, that he, more perhaps than any other that preceded or came after him, had sought to find support on what would prove resistance.

I WOULD NOT in the least disturb the faith of genuine piety that venerates the Master of the Gospels as the only "son of God."

Those who hold to this belief, and in it hope to find salvation, may feel assured their faith will not deceive them, provided they allow the Master's teachings to gain life in them.

They also may be certain that the blessings they are able to receive will never be dependent on their views concerning the events that once had led to the appearance of the Master here on earth.

If their faith is strong, they should not hesitate to read what here will be presented; and anything that might unsettle the roots of their belief, they simply ought to disregard.

The greater the strength of their faith is in truth, the more surely will they draw new energies from these disclosures; for "Anyone who has, shall be given more that he may have in abundance." If they feel weak and uncertain, however, and if their faith serves them merely as a feeble consolation, offered them by teachers who themselves are often wracked by doubt, but feel condemned by duty to provide, then they would do well to read no further; for it is also written, "From him who does not have will be taken away even what he *thinks* he has."

Others, however, who feel inclined to look upon the teachings on eternal life presented by the rabbi Yehoshua of Nazareth, radiant in sacred love, merely as a pious legend, or even doubt the God-united teacher actually existed, may here acquaint themselves with some realities concerning him which are disclosed to those whose *Brother* and appointed messenger he was; he, of whom it was recorded that he taught "unlike" the teachers of his time; that he spoke like one "who had authority," simply because, in full awareness of his essence, he could not speak in other terms if he were not to be untrue to his own self.

However much the records that describe his life and teachings had to absorb of mystical additions, they nonetheless still offer more of factual reality to be considered than rationalistic criticism, unaware of more profound relationships, is able to accept when judging merely from without.

THE LIFE and teachings of this man, who had become, for now almost two thousand years, a "God" to nations in the West, will never be discerned in all its depth by purely philological research of sources; nor is the building that arose as "Christendom" upon this life and on these teachings, so empty of transparent symbols of profoundest insight, notwithstanding some abstruse formations, as some of its despisers naively seem to think.

To be sure, one must not view the cleansing which the honest, energetic Augustinian monk of Wittenberg, imbued with simple-hearted piety, had sought to bring about in his own way to have been a complete success, and valid for all time. One should not, blinded by pure veneration, grant his homespun peasant faith in God, and notions of the Devil, that high degree of spiritual insight that would have been required to carry through a genuine "Reformation," while carefully preserving timeless symbols, whose depth, however, he was not able to discern.

The work that he believed to have accomplished is yet to be achieved one day; and it will have to be performed in ways that differ from the one that he, for all the power of his lofty will, was able to pursue.

His task, however, was to break the ground that will provide the solid basis for him who one day shall achieve that work, enlightened by profoundest knowledge.

Then only shall the deepest mysteries of Christendom, unearthed again from shafts obstructed by debris, make lucid sense to all mankind, so that their light may finally illuminate the darkness, which for many had obscured the path that long ago the Master of Nazareth had cleared within himself for all who were resolved to follow him.

Then only will one understand the reason why this messenger of love and wisdom truly had the right to say to those he called his own, "Apart from me, you can do nothing."

And why he called himself the "vine," and those who were his own the "branches"; why he declared that all who wanted to have life within had to receive within themselves even what in his own person had gained form as "flesh and blood."

HERE, INDEED, is wisdom of profound perception; however, it will not be found unless one knows about the nature of this "son of Man," and whence he came. Those who fully grasped these facts will in the end discover with amazement that ancient "dogma" will not be by any means uprooted by the truth.

Those who through the centuries believed they needed to protect it, never fathomed that the roots of "dogma" anchor at far deeper levels than their faith can reach; nor do they realize today that underneath the shifting sands of theological conjectures, which they incessantly re-sift, there lies eternal, rich and fertile soil; but this they are unable to discover merely because they never tire of the fruitless game of drawing magic symbols on the surface of the sand, in the belief that solely through the hidden power of such symbols could the liberation be accomplished which the Master once had promised unto all who seek to unify themselves in him.

To CHRISTIAN believers, there only is a single "one-begotten Son of the Father," namely the Master after whom they name themselves; even though the Master himself, "full of grace and truth," declared that there are "many mansions" in his Father's house, but that it was not his to grant who would "sit at his right hand and his left," in his Father's kingdom, and that the Father was "greater" than he.

"Even though I bear witness of myself, my witness is true; for I know where I have come from and where I go; but you do not know where I come from, nor where I go."

And likewise to this day no quest of thought nor faith will apprehend him clearly in his essential individuation unless those thinking and believing comprehended where the Master "came from" and would also "go"; unless they knew that here they stand before a *Luminary of eternal Light*, venerated and admired by his *Brothers* to this very hour as the Lord of Love among them, having gone forth from their midst, to which he had returned again, dedicated not to leave the spiritual aura of this earth, in bodily invisible form, until the last of human spirits that here are born in animal bondage has once again entered the dimension of light.

Everything that any of these *Luminaries of eternal Light* may say about his person when "bearing witness of himself," he states as one who represents the timeless spiritual body, unifying many, whereof he is a part. He thus speaks at the same time of himself, as likewise of all others who, in unity with him, comprise the *Luminaries of eternal Light*.

But for the existence of this *com-unity* within the cosmos of the Spirit, the *spiritual human being*, which, owing to its self-willed "Fall," had strayed into a different "dimension," would long ago have fallen prey to everlasting night, lost in its animal embodiment, its only true, because eternal, "death"—the dissolution of its individuated spiritual consciousness; the return into the unformed "chaos," into the Ground of Being's endless night, from whose eternally self-generating form it once had risen, endowed with form, as life "begotten" not "created."

Eternal Love, ablaze within the midst of primal "chaos," like a fiery source of radiant light surpassing comprehension—timeless *primordial Light*—gives voice to its Self as the *primordial Word*, in echoes of infinite number, perceiving its Self manifested in numberless forms of its Being.

That is how "the *Word* of the Lord goes out to the ends of the earth"; and in each of its *Words* it becomes its own "answer" and worship; in each it appears as the blazing "sun" that of itself begets the system of its "planets"—the individuated "Godhead" of the individual within the Spirit, whom of itself it brings forth without end.

Within this "heart of God"—the center of all Being's radiant Light, the wellspring inside formless "chaos," which no word of human language comprehends, unless one were to name it "Love in Being through itself,"—the "plan of man's salvation," has its roots. Founded on Love from eternity, it created the Oneness of *Luminaries,* whose members are many, that it may rescue what appears to be lost, and once more return to the bliss of its conscious existence what had scattered itself, and thereby abandoned the conscious awareness of its own form.

Having no choice but to speak in temporal images, I know quite well there will be some, proud and certain of their knowledge based on mental concepts, who will reject the like occurring in the realm that is eternal as "absurd"; however, that which is *eternal* in *reality* is something very different from concepts of the intellect's imagination; and no wisdom of the mortal mind will ever mold the concept that here conforms with what is truly *real.*

Only in their feeling's inmost depth may seekers "of good will" discern a glimpse of that which in reality comprises the *eternal,* and all attempts of rational speculations are doomed to founder on the rocks of that reality.

Among all those who live on earth, only one who has "found back" to where he once had come from, in his spiritual identity, can ever bear authentic witness of that ultimate reality.

"No one comes to the Father, but through me."

He that once had spoken that word belonged among the very few who had experienced that reality, and knew it "face to face," long before they found a human creature's mortal garb on earth, through which embodiment they thus could teach the things the Father told them to make known.

Each of the *Luminaries of primordial Light*, but only one who, owing to the call and mission of *primordial Light* effectively belongs among their number, may use the same word as relating to himself, and with the selfsame meaning, based upon the likeness of his spiritual essence with that of the Master who is recorded to have said that word; even so, however, all his *Brothers* venerate in him the one who by his radiant might of Love exceeded all who ever walked on earth as human beings.

However much each one that through the ages did belong to that community embodied Love in his own life, there never has been any who so completely offered his entire self, transfigured by the might of Love, to all the world as radiant, living help as he had done whom they themselves have named the Lord of Love.

Very few have ever grasped what he bestowed on all of humankind.

His deed so far exceeds all bounds of human comprehension that those who first divined the magnitude of what he had accomplished could not help but think he was a "God," lest such surpassing greatness of a *human being* should wholly crush the sense of their own worthiness.

Yet his work of liberation has no need of any myth that fantasizes of a vengeance-driven tribal God who sent his "son" to mankind as a human being so that his own vindictiveness would find its satisfaction through their cruelty.

What the Lord of Love had offered mankind as a heritage from the dominion of the Spirit was likewise something altogether different from the "vicarious atonement" invented by the wish for effortless salvation that feels no longer any need for personal endeavor and commitment.

Upon the cross of Golgotha the world was truly "freed" from bondage, albeit in a way profoundly different from that believed by those who dimly sensed the truth.

WHEN, ON THE gibbet of the Roman cross, the Master of Nazareth finally suffered the death that in his highest hours he had always sought, he performed a deed incomparably greater than anything that all before or after him had done who sacrificed their lives on earth to their convictions.

He that died upon the cross at Golgotha was at that sacred place the only one who was aware in total clarity of the events that were unfolding; nor was there anyone but he alone who had the power, by virtue of the Love that he released in death, to break the chains by which the gate to freedom had been locked for human spirits from the time that, born in animal bodies on earth, they had so thoroughly succumbed to the creature's drives and instincts that a *redemption* from the fate of animal nature appeared no longer possible.

Only one endowed with final knowledge was capable of recognizing that a human being's highest sacrifice of Love was able not only once more to awaken a spiritual power within the realm of human might, but to awaken it in such a way that it would be accessible to all who were in danger of being suffocated by the animal's proliferating creature instincts; and, furthermore, that only one who had united his spiritual essence with the animal, thus bringing forth a new existence, could open that path to freedom for all who were prepared to follow him.

Yet he that had such knowledge would at the same time have to be empowered with a might of Love beyond all measure in order to be able to perform the deed he could envision; for many who had lived before him shared that very knowledge, but even so could not surmount the horror of the deed, although they, too, were surely vessels of eternal Love.

AND THUS the path to the Spirit had been unlocked by Jesus of Nazareth and opened for all who are willing to bring to life within themselves what was alive in him.

In him, the God within the animal had unified the animal with his own self, begetting that new being he used to speak of as the *Son of Man*; the "son" begotten by the human spirit in the animal, when it has overcome the animal in which it was imprisoned, by letting it behold its own magnificence and power.

Although the same awareness is shared by every *Luminary of primordial Light*, none had found within himself that might of Love beyond all measure that would have moved him now also to perform the deed through which the Master of Nazareth had brought an energy to life again, which to attain the wisest had since ancient times devoted all their lives, but without being able to make it equally accessible to others.

It was not his death as such that brought about the restoration of that energy within the spiritual aura of the earth, nor was it reawakened by the torture that preceded the Master's death.

Love was the power that alone accomplished this wonder.

That he, compelled to suffer torture and death, was able to *forgive* humanity, was moved by *forgiveness* to his final breath, that alone was his work of enduring *redemption*; for in accord with spiritual law, this brought about that human spirits, wherever they may live on earth and, in bondage to the animal, had burdened themselves with guilt, were freed from their subservience by the might of Love—if only they will grasp the hand that reaches out to help them; if they will but receive within them that which in the *Luminary* had gained form as "flesh and blood," so that they may unite the animal with their own spirit in themselves.

Only one to whom "the Father had entrusted everything" could bring a *forgiveness* whose effects would embrace all of humanity.

Ageless wisdom found concealment in the garb of myth that, according to ancient tradition, has the Master "descend," after his death on the cross, to the souls of the just of earlier ages; because the consequences of his deed are not confined within the bounds of time, but can be felt by those who had lived on earth long ago, and likewise by all yet to be born in millennia to come.

MUCH THAT here is to be said may well seem tedious banality to those who only will accept ·as fact what they able to perceive by means of senses shared with other animals.

They are unable, in the true sense of the word, to "grasp" the concept that the action of a single human being could have completely altered the spiritual potential for everything that bears the name of "human."

Those who are unable, or unwilling, to consider what I here explain, I truly have no inclination to "convert."

I merely would remind them of the debt which countless millions owe to single individuals in fields that all can apprehend by virtue of their creature senses.

How much farther reaching still become the actions of a single individual who is empowered to effect events out of the Spirit, admittedly remains beyond the sight of mortal eyes. Only they can apprehend a small part of these consequences who likewise have received the task of being active in and from the Spirit's realm.

But all who, guided by their deepest inner feelings, behold the Master of Nazareth as the sublime creator of a work no other ever has accomplished for all of humankind, let them search their souls and ask themselves in an hour of sacred reflection whether they likewise are willing to benefit from the fruits of that work by a deed of their own: by uniting themselves with the power the Master had once more awakened; by wresting themselves from the conflict between their animal lives and the Godhead; by receiving within, in vigor and truth, what in their Master had come to be "flesh and blood," so that it also may within themselves bring forth the union of their earthly human being with the Godhead's life.

Many a noble deed of great and powerful mortals has through the ages faded from human memory, but even the most distant future generations of this planet shall know about the mystery of Golgotha. Indeed, it is to be hoped they shall be far more conscious of its gifts than these were able to reveal themselves until this day.

As a radiant beacon of compassion that surpasses every measure, this Gospel prayer sends its light through all the ages, "Father, forgive them; for they know not what they do."

None but a *Luminary of primordial Light* was able to utter that word; yet none of them dared to accomplish the deed that was its condition, excepting the one, the *Lord of Love*.

Even today, as to the end of human existence on earth, this Lord of Love—one with all others who, like himself, create the spiritual chain that links the world of physical senses, which passes away, with the realm that endures forever—is close to the souls that call him.

"Let those who are capable grasp it!"

The present writer bears witness of him, even as he could of the sun.

No MEMBER of the Oneness embodying many, composed of the *Luminaries of primordial Light*, is ever separated from the other members of this spiritual community, and none will act on his account alone.

Even he that, almost two thousand years ago, combining power and compassion, brought "glad tidings" to his all too simple-minded pupils, effects events today, as he did then, at no time solely on his own.

He, too, obeys the call that reaches him, like all his *Brothers*, from the *primordial Word*, whose *Words* are all who, one with him, effect events on earth.

He, too, is subject to the *Father*, the timeless Being in the Spirit, sublime beyond all comprehension who is in truth the real *Master* in every *Luminary of primordial Light*; the sacred sovereign of all the *Brothers* active here on earth; the One without name who is as He is through all eternities; abiding in the *Word of the Beginning*, and yet continuously present in His spiritual form to every *Luminary* here on earth, revealed to their sight, and, according to the gifts and faculties of each, advancing the work of Love without end.

UNIFIED WITHIN that One no word can name, in whom the first self-recognition of the *primordial Word* becomes both form and its effect— as the Word that is "with God," and which is "God" within the "Godhead"—all the *Luminaries of primordial Light* remain eternally united as a single will and consciousness.

ONENESS IS the capstone and the crown of fundamental multiplicity in all of life within the cosmos of the Spirit's realm; even as a multitude of colors, when unified, appears as purest white.

The One that is the All reveals itself in manifold infinities, in order to unite itself again in Oneness, while never sacrificing its infinity.

Love is the innermost source of its Being.

Love is its life without end.

Love is its work never ceasing.

He that died at Golgotha, however, was the most consummate vessel of this Love that ever had offered itself on this earth—the Love whose bounds are endless, although it knows its limits in itself.

Blest are all who recognize his words, though buried under layers of debris,

Blest are all who in their heart of hearts will know the way to find him.

☙

CHAPTER TWO

THE MOST PERNICIOUS OF OUR FOES

HERE I AM NOT SPEAKING OF THE horrible external wars, which time and again the animal part in earthly human beings will readily unleash to slaughter its own kind; I rather have in mind a far more cruel war, which can break out in every human mortal, and then may rage within that person's inner life; a war in which not many are able to claim victory.

That war begins when first the human mind confronts the question, "Who am I?" When first that questioning "I," which has no knowledge of itself peers down the greedy, yawning jaws of a seemingly impenetrable darkness as it searches for the purpose or the cause of its existence, for traces of its origins, and glimpses of its final destination.

Accustomed to solving all questions by mental effort, it never occurs to human beings that the key to answering the questions that have now arisen might lie in the hands of a different, but *spiritual* capacity within them.

To be sure, souls that are weary or averse to exertion soon enough find a solution, which they call their "faith." That concept of "faith," however, is merely a shallow, more easily found pacification of a modest mind; it is not the sublime energy, which those possessing insight have revered through the ages when they spoke of *faith*.

Instead, the mind will there content itself with a solution it accepted second hand, because it is incapable of reaching an answer of its own.

One could fill colossal libraries with all the books that thinkers wrote to pacify their minds; apart from the personal endeavors of those who quelled their minds by accepting such second-hand appeasement, and thus feel duty-bound to preach "salvation," of the kind they think they found, likewise to their fellow mortals.

Yet in this way one never can teach more than what the mind will comprehend; and if the intellect could undertake to solve those final questions, the solution would have long ago been found for all the world to see in perfect clarity.

The intellect, however, is to serve the human being merely as a tool. It never must become the master of its owner, or it will prove the human being's most pernicious foe.

THE DIAMOND serves well for cutting glass, but to fell trees it is useless; and one who needs wood to build himself a solid house can freeze to death with his diamond in the blizzards of winter.

You search for answers with your intellect, berating nature as cruel because she did not give you the eye one needs to discover her final, most secretive depths; while you in truth are granted that eye, but in all of your wealth do not know it.

In every age have lived some human beings on this earth who knew about that inner eye and had the gift to use it.

When they revealed to others, such as you, what they beheld, they were reviled as fools and dreamers, and their names became discredited.

But if they offered you advice how you might find and use that inner eye yourselves, you found them to be troublesome; because what they demanded of you was too much, which little pleased your indolence.

Instead, you rather "believed" in the teachings of those possessing knowledge after you had nailed those teachers on the cross; for then you could make use of their words at your pleasure.

You TELL me, "Others did such things—not we!—not we!"—but I have valid reasons to doubt that you today would recognize the teachers who could help you.

Humans in all ages rather waited for the coming of a future helper according to their own ideas, and did not want to hear about the real helpers, who offered them their hands in kindness and without pretensions.

The human mind created mighty "titans," "Gods," and "saints," while of all human beings the most human alone is able to free them from bondage.

The magical aura of conjurers has always been held in higher esteem than the profoundest teachings of those who truly taught with authority.

One craves amazement and wants to stand in awe; indeed, would love to become a "sorcerer's apprentice," when instead one's goal should be to find oneself, in silence and inner reflection.

In short, the "method" of making this inner eye capable of seeing appears to the fantasy-prone inclination of mortals as far too simple; and thus it goes against their grain to think that lasting knowledge could be gained in such a new and unromantic way.

Too long have humans lived in bondage to their intellect to be able still to fathom that one can walk without the weight of leaden chains around one's legs; and, sad to say, ascending on the wings of the soul they have forgotten long ago.

In outer life, the thinking mind provides a feeble substitute for everything the soul may seek, making humans stand in awe before the "miracles" the intellect has helped them to bring forth; and so they lose the last remaining faith in ever being able on their own to still the longing of the soul—by virtue of the soul.

Yet nothing that the mind lets human beings apprehend within external life can wholly stifle the scream of the soul, which in her own realm is no less entitled to her rights than is the mind in the domain where only mental comprehension has its place.

The insights of the soul would not be "understood," but *felt, experienced, viewed,* and *conquered.*

In this, the intellect, however sharply honed its edge might be, is useless as a tool.

A new and different energy must here come into action; it is one that every human being essentially possesses, although a tiny number only will unfold it in themselves.

There is no word to signify this energy, and those who had developed it invented merely "names" that shed no light on it for others.

"Emotional sensitivity" perhaps may lead most closely to the realm in which at times a glimpse can be perceived, but one associates so many nebulous conceptions with that term that even this slight hint may lead to serious error.

HERE I SHALL attempt, employing various images, to guide the soul with utmost care to a perception of that energy. Perhaps one reader or another will feel that something gently comes to life within, which, even as a seed its flower, will one day bring that energy to light.

Still, I know the task I face can never be successfully accomplished unless there is, on either side, the earnest and determined will to reach the goal, ignoring every hindrance.

The most pernicious foe we may encounter on that path, however, is the intellect—that relentless, habitually ingrained attempt to "understand" the goal, while here one can at most seek understanding of the words that would direct the reader toward the goal.

Let those who would come with me any farther above all else subordinate their intellect, conceding it no rights where its effectiveness has ended.

But how shall I unveil to you the essence of this nameless power, which is to grant you liberation?

Attempt to read these words again and again, far from all the noises and distractions of the outer world; but also seek to calm your mind and shield it from the loud intrusions of your thinking; and now in utmost peacefulness grow conscious of your self-aware, clearheaded feelings.

When reading what is here suggested, attempt in silence to be conscious of your self.

The feeling you should try to reach resembles that when, unexpectedly at twilight of a peaceful day, you faintly in the distance hear a melody you once had loved, but never heard since then, which now lays hold of you, and on its wings of gentle sounds will carry you aloft.

In such hours, at such moments, a brief opening is seen at the portal through which you one day need to pass if you truly want to approach the power that will answer the questions you harbor on *final things*.

Welcome the gentle ray of light escaping through the portal, behold it with a loving eye and seek to grow accustomed to its mellow gleam.

Do not endeavor all at once to apprehend the full abundance of the brightness found beyond the portal, but firmly curb your wishes, and first allow your eye to learn how to distinguish the nature of that gentle light from any other kind of radiance.

You then will soon discover that until now you have neglected something in yourself that would have been well worth the effort to be nurtured.

Come out with me into open nature. Not in the noisy bustle at noon, although even the hour "when Great Pan is sleeping" abounds in mysteries for those who are able to feel them, but late in the evening, when the clamor of the day has come to rest, or in the early morning before sunrise.

You then will sense a presence in the wide expanse that lifts your heart in silent joy, independent of all thinking, or reasons of the mind.

Surrender yourself to that feeling and let its roots find ground in you.

Repeat that experience often, to make yourself familiar with what your feel within.

Learn clearly to distinguish its subtleties and shadings.

It is not the same whether you merely recreate these feelings in your room, or rather experience them freshly in the open air, each time anew and directly.

Your room, whatever its appearance, will have its own distinctive atmosphere, and even if your memory allows you to recall most clearly what you wish, you unintentionally are bound to falsify the feeling you would recreate.

INDOORS YOU will have other means to "tune" your inner self, so that your soul's most secret strings may fill your being with their sound.

Music, paintings, sculptures, no less than works of poetry, can let you find yourself within.

But whether you might be outdoors, on the peak of a mountain, or at the banks of a peaceful river; whether you seek to be moved by the endless expanse of the sea, or by the light of a lamp will read and experience the words of a poet—in every setting it will be your inner self that apprehends emotion; because all things outside are no more than the cause that generates vibrations; they do not in themselves contain what, through their mediation, your soul is apt to feel.

The wonders of nature remain lifeless and cold, and every work of art can be viewed without feelings if your own soul is devoid of the conscious potential that nature and art would stir in your being.

Within yourself alone you find the magic well that fills your golden goblets.

Thus you have already come a measurable distance closer to the energy one cannot name.

You come to learn that you can "tune" your inner self; and everything—including food and clothing, the places you seek out, as well as solitude and company—may thus in time become a kind of "tuning fork."

According to the way you "tuned" yourself, you will cause different chords to sound within you; and soon you will discover which particular attunement most closely meets your quest for inner clarity.

Already you are working with that nameless energy; yet what you so far learned to master, and make it serve your ends, are but its darkest and most distant rays.

But here one can go farther, continue to ascend, and enter the realm of absolute clarity.

Those who would advance this way must make their lives a work of art.

What they had once regarded as "fulfillment," they now must view as only "raw material," from which, like sculptors, they will shape their souls' consummate structure.

Not haphazardly, or subject purely to their mood, can they any longer let themselves be governed by whatever life may hold in store for them.

They themselves must learn to shape and govern their own lives, by means of their ability to "tune" themselves at any moment according to the spirit of their highest goal.

Until here will many readers have been able to follow me, but at this point shall the majority give up; for in their judgment it surpasses human powers in this way to master all the events and burdens of everyday existence.

Only the few that are mature enough will here not fail the challenge.

And they alone shall also on this way at last within themselves detect the energy which those must first have learned to master who seek to benefit from entering the path to timeless light, prepared for them by Masters from that realm.

From the day a human being will discover and learn to use this inner energy, that seeker shall begin a new and different life, compared to which all "life" as known before will seem like clouded dawn when set against the brilliant summer sun at noon.

And yet, this day will find the human being merely at the threshold of the path that leads to timeless Light; the path that has no end as it ascends from clarity to clarity; where every level of perception continues to be still surpassed by a profounder, purer, new degree of insight, which once again gives way to higher comprehension, more bountiful experience, and more lucid apprehending.

This path is endless as its goal is without end, and can be contemplated in infinitely varied ways; it is endless because its goal contains infinities, and could not ever be entirely explored, not even in a billion aeons.

But none shall ever find this path who has not first discovered that nameless inner energy, that spiritual eye, of which throughout the ages the wisest mortals spoke in more or less transparent symbols; that inner eye, which even sees in regions where the light of our earthly sun is swallowed by a brighter light, as a spark will vanish in a fiery blaze.

None will ever find that eye within, nor learn its use for seeing, who lets himself be blinded by the pyrotechnics of the intellect; none who let the intellect—within its realm a useful tool —become his lord and master and, thus, his most pernicious foe.

Knowing this from timeless self-experience, the Master thanks the One he speaks of as the *Father* that he reveals himself to the "little ones" and the unschooled, but stays hidden from those who are the slaves of what they merely learned.

And with deepest knowledge he speaks about the "little ones," like whom all those need to become who seek to encounter "the kingdom of heaven" in themselves.

About himself, the callous hearts who heard him wondered, "How is it that this man has such learning, never having studied scripture?"

They did not sense that he could draw from a far deeper source of wisdom in himself than ever "scripture" did reveal to the learned in Holy Writ, who labored as slaves of the mind because they had found nothing within them but the intellect; nothing that could have offered them light of a higher kind, and clarity more comprehensive.

It will be the first and foremost, all other aims surpassing task of future generations to make the spiritual source of wisdom, deeply hidden in each human being, fruitful for the benefit of earthly life; quite apart from what the treasures of true knowledge gathered from that source will bring about within the soul's immortal life, once it is free of its temporal body.

But not until the courage is awakened to get rid of all the rubbish that intellectual arrogance has diligently heaped upon that source through the millennia, will human beings on this earth be able once again to find that wellspring in themselves, in depths of inmost feeling they scarcely can conceive today.

❧

CHAPTER THREE

LOVE AND HATRED

"**L**OVE YOUR ENEMIES, DO GOOD TO them that hate you!"

It is extremely difficult to keep such a commandment as long as only feelings of bad conscience will prod one to a sense of love.

Even as a person with good breeding will naturally and freely exhibit pleasant manners, while another, who dismisses mannerly behavior as a burdensome annoyance, displays himself to be an awkward churl if he should find himself in well-bred company—so, too, will only those be able to feel love with unforced spontaneity who made the art of life, which is an art of love, so thoroughly their own that it has mastered flesh and blood.

Where flesh and blood are not yet mastered by the art of life, all the love induced by force, in order to comply with a commandment, remains a wretched grimace, and must become a "sin" against one's flesh and blood; a lie that drains the marrow of one's life.

Thousands feel an inner "duty" forces them to live that lie against themselves, wholly unaware that they would be far better off if they could harbor feelings of hostility and hatred without a guilty conscience.

They would appear more virtuous in their own judgment than they are; and thereby will themselves obstruct the path on which they one day might grow able—in truthfulness, spontaneously, and without effort—to act according to the commandment, which only fear of guilt makes them obey with reluctance.

Beclouded understanding here pursues mistaken ways.

While those who follow this mistaken way had sought to learn how Love is to be loved, they instead are merely hating hatred.

But hatred only is the form of energy that is devoid—not conscious—of its might; the selfsame energy that, in the form of Love, finds liberation in itself.

Whoever can still hate the force of hatred has not yet known the might of Love; but those who never could feel hatred, will likewise never learn to love.

DEEPLY ANCHORED in the dark of the primordial abyss abides the power that, transfigured in its godlike form, reveals itself as Love; and in those depths it likewise generates its polar opposite, the energy of hatred.

Hatred and Love are aspects of one essence; much as the root beneath a stalk of wheat shares its essence with the ear above, which offers wholesome food to humans.

But even as between the root and ear above, the stalk ascends with more than one connecting link, so are there likewise many intermittent levels on the path that leads from the instinctive, lower drive toward feeling hatred, to that selfsame power's closeness to the realm of God—to Love unfolding its omnipotence.

None of these transitional levels must be "skipped" if one would truly learn the art of Love by practice.

Perhaps you only have arrived at one such intermittent state?

Perhaps you still are not yet capable of Love in its consummate, truest form?

Let this not weigh upon your mind, nor seek to accomplish anything by force.

Ask, instead, within yourself for the gift of grace from above that the power which commands you still to hate, may soon reveal itself to you in its divine, most radiant form—as Love.

Thus only can you one day truly know the might of Love within you; and then you surely will no longer harbor hate, the low expression of that selfsame power; nor shall you henceforth meet that force with hatred.

So long as love still needs an object it can hate, and though it were the most despicable of things, whatever you call "love" is but a changeling of betrayed pursuits and feelings, which does not have the least in common with Love of godlike power.

In your future, higher spiritual life, having begun to ascend, when after the death of the animal body that served you, you live freely in spiritual bodily form, you will not even be able to hate; for nothing enters life in the infinite realms of pure Spirit that ever could waken your hatred.

But here on earth, as long as you still live within an earthly creature body, there is much that would mislead you to feel hate.

Yet never shall your hatred serve you on the way to your own self; the path that leads you back to your primordial home; to the truth of timeless life within the heart of Godhead, as a purely spiritual being, a "son of God" in the dimension of pure Spirit, in the "Father of Lights," in whom abide the bliss and fullness of all Life throughout the aeons without end.

When you harbor hatred in yourself, even if you feel you only hate what should be hated, you always shall defraud yourself by not unfolding the highest of your inner powers, the radiant might of Love.

Although from timeless Light you once had fallen far into the deep, so that you now must live embodied in a mortal earthly creature, that godlike energy pervades you even here; but you alone determine whether you employ that power, such as it remains in you, to manifest its godlike, radiant form as Love, or instead transform that might into its polar opposite, restricted merely to the life of lower "nature," pervading the immeasurable physical universe, where it is active both in its invisible entities, and equally in human beings, whose mortal forms your earthly eyes are able to perceive.

THERE TRULY are invisible intelligences in this universe that only live for hatred's sake, but even them you must not hate, however much their hatred might besiege you.

You can emerge as victor only if you confront them with a love that paralyzes even their most fiendish hatred, so that they must fall back and turn from you because your love would make them suffer pain.

You may despise whatever is despicable; that is to say, deny its worthlessness respect, but you must not assume you therefore need to hate it.

The moment you begin to hate, you connect yourself with all the entities throughout this physical universe, who, owing to their nature, experience that primordial cosmic power solely in the form of hatred, and who never will be able to transform it into Love.

You thus will reinforce the streams of hatred which, through them, are made to flow into the hearts of humans; you make yourself guilty of all things destructive that hatred begets among mortals on earth; and thus you follow the road that leads to destruction, to the abyss, instead of raising yourself to pursue your ascent.

THE POWERFUL, invisible intelligences within nature's physical universe, whose lives are limited by time, although that span may number thousands of years, are constantly determined to possess you, because they cannot ever apprehend the Spirit's world, and thus consider you exclusively as their own subject.

Not all of them are to the same degree controlled by hatred, and there are some indeed who honestly believe that they protect you from an error when they try to hold you back from your ascent to the domain of Spirit, and seek to keep you bound to their own sphere of power.

You need to recognize that, owing to the might of Love, which to the very best of them remains unknown, even while they are not thralls of hatred, you are more powerful than they by far.

You need to know that, in respect to your physical intelligence, your rank is far below the majority of these great powers; and also, that your thinking is subjected in a high degree to their compelling influence; but that despite this you are able, thanks to your inherent spiritual nature, to attain a timeless kind of knowledge that remains forever barred to their experience, because they cannot ever apprehend the Spirit, given that they are themselves not of the Spirit, which thus cannot reveal its Being to their knowledge, however all-surpassing it may be; much as you yourself are never able to reveal the fullness of your thoughts and feelings to any animal on earth.

Be not deceived and venerate whatever may surpass your powers!

One thing alone is worthy of your veneration, of lifting your eyes with longing to what is above, and that one thing transcends the whole of physical nature's universe with its legions of mighty wielders of power and lofty intelligences beyond the grasp of our mortal senses.

Your primordial home in the realm of the Spirit is the only goal toward which you ought to lift your eyes with longing, and that great goal you can attain if Love inspires your life.

At Golgotha has Love been liberated of its fetters by compassion's purest vessel.

Whether or not you belong to those who call themselves "Christians," given he was a "Christos"—one anointed in eternal consecration—you partake of the power that he liberated only if you offer Love the space and means to manifest itself in your own life.

Devoid of Love you never will achieve your liberation.

The Love of Being's inmost Sun of Love had called you forth, eternities ago, and only Love shall also lead you back once more to your primordial origin.

❧

CHAPTER FOUR

THE SOUL AND ITS GROWTH

ONE HAS GOOD REASON TO SPEAK OF the "growth of the soul," because the "soul," as I have sufficiently explained in other contexts, is an organism that only our highest inner senses are able to perceive, consisting of innumerable energies, the *elements that form the soul*, which Indian terminology, correctly understood, refers to as the "skandhas."

In a cadaver on the dissecting table no surgeon will detect the soul, but in himself he surely may, provided he did not allow his inner sense of self to wither.

The soul is capable of growth, but it can also be diminished; indeed, it may be nearly lost already during life on earth, without thereby disabling the functions of the body's organs.

The soul can also cease to grow, or suffer symptoms of sterility, effectively preventing any further growth.

Not without good reason does religious faith admonish its believers, "Save your souls!"

For "What would a man benefit if he gained the whole world, but did harm to his soul?"

YES, ONE'S SOUL can truly suffer harm, and very many harm their souls without giving it the slightest thought; indeed, they often may feel certain that their souls are in the midst of growing, yet do not realize that what they take to be their "soul" is no more than the subtler, invisible organism that is part of the material physical body; an organism that can surely be of very beneficial use if it is guided by the soul's dynamic elements, and thus becomes the servant of the soul; but which can also fatally obstruct the workings of the soul if self-importantly it gains supremacy within a human being.

All those who seek to redirect their souls' demands, which commonly one calls "religious" feeling, and instead find their "religion" in, for instance, the world of the arts, in the culture of aestheticism, in the pursuit of scientific knowledge, or in the love of "nature," are slaves of this subtler physical organism and in serious danger of murdering their souls.

Even though some of the elements that form their souls may still be at work in them, they are unable to unify these elements into an *individuated conscious soul*; and when some day not only the physical body, but also its subtler energies will be taken from them, they will be compelled to spend "millennia," by earthly counting, in a dull, tormenting semi-consciousness before their helpers from above are able once more to "awaken" their souls, in order that "awakened" they truly may begin to live where only those can live in fullest clarity of consciousness in whom the soul's dynamic elements have unified themselves into an individuated conscious self.

THEREFORE IT was said, "Work, for the night is coming when none will be able to work."

That night will come for only those, however, who did not knowingly increase the treasure of their souls' dynamic energies, entrusted to them here on earth.

"To each that has shall more be given that he may have in abundance, but from him that does not have shall be taken away even what he may think he has, no matter how little."

Whoever, like the "faithful servant," knows how to increase what he has received from his master, of him it is said, "Because you have been faithful over a few things, I shall make you ruler over many things."

But one who buries his pound and only returns what he received at the beginning, that mortal, according to eternal laws, shall be forced to encounter "outer darkness," the realm devoid of the soul's every warmth, where "weeping and gnashing of teeth" result from coldness of heart and anguish.

THE SAYINGS of the Gospels cited here present no more than the effectiveness of spiritual laws, expressed in vivid images.

What is experienced through the body, we also can perceive without the soul; even though perceiving through the body, but guided by the soul, results in impressions of consciousness that differ substantially from those which the body's the subtler physical faculties are able to transmit.

The popular belief that the material body cannot exist without a "soul," here wrongly takes those subtler, fluidic, physical energies to be the "soul," while at the same time it attributes qualities to those physical energies which in truth belong exclusively to the eternal soul.

If only the body, having lost its soul, were lifeless as well! For then the many who have forfeited their soul would not deprive this earthly life of its warmth, and the warning of the Gospel would be groundless.

But while in fact the body retains its consciousness, even devoid of a soul; and while also a human who has lost his soul is conscious of his being as a bodily determined *self*, as in the understanding of Max Stirner, it is absolutely impossible for us to apprehend the realm that is pure Spirit—the objectively existing spiritual dimensions—except by virtue of the soul.

THE ONLY *self* that also in this realm is capable of apprehending is equally an element from the domain of the soul, but one that is for all eternity illuminated and imbued with life by a scintilla of the Spirit's timeless light, when, in the course of its awakening, it recognizes its potential of becoming that scintilla's radiant spiritual "body"; when, in other words, the *living God* was able to bring forth his *birth* within that mortal's *self*.

All the soul's dynamic elements must crystallize around that *self*; and with that *self* must all of them be unified if any human being is to be able to enter realm of the eternal Spirit's radiant substance as a fully conscious individuation.

The concept "spirit," in ordinary usage, comprises mental disposition, impulse, mood, vitality, and temperament.

These qualities are products of the subtler physical energies concealed within the human being's mortal body.

The "spirit" of such everyday usage has nothing whatever in common with the dimension of the timeless Spirit's living substance, which I here discuss; no more so than the "soul" that one ascribes to animals has anything at all to do with the dynamic energies that form the ever flowing ocean of the soul, when here I speak about the "growth" the human soul is able to attain.

There are numerous emotional sensations, presumed to be due to the "soul," found in the human being's animal body as well; and in some it is far surpassed by other animals; but this "soul" of the animal, which is a natural component also of the human organism, will neither make the human being, nor the animal, capable of apprehending the dimension of the Spirit; even as the most highly developed intellect proves useless for attaining consciousness in the dimension of the Spirit's radiant substance.

One is too readily deceived by the fact that, during our physical life, the brain becomes the transformer for every type of sensation, so that not only the effects of the subtler physical energies of the body—whether mistakenly seen as "spiritual," or ascribed to the "soul," —but also the genuine experience of the eternal realm of the soul, and of the Spirit's dimension, are constantly recorded by the brain, as long as there exists a healthy living brain.

But even though quite different sensations are here recorded by the identical instrument, one must not for that reason fail to differentiate, but rather learn to recognize within oneself the nature of sensation that in a given case seeks to impress the mental apparatus.

If one earnestly cares to further the growth of the soul, it must at all events become one's foremost goal to make the brain so sensitive for every genuine sensation of the soul, for every contact by its energies, that none of its vibrations will be missed.

To that end it is by no means necessary, nor would it be completely possible, to blunt the brain's receptiveness for other sense impressions; for during our life on earth both the functions of the body's subtler physical energies, as well as those of coarser nature, are important and thus should not escape the brain's continued watchfulness.

But, "Seek ye first the kingdom of God, and" —what it demands—"its justness"—following the proper fulfillment of eternal laws—"and everything else shall be added unto you."

It betrays a serious failing to assume that one could benefit the life of the soul only by fleeing "the wicked world with all its conflicts," so that one can be certain to escape all interruptions.

Only by constant practice, and efforts to conquer resistance, can the physical body's potential gain strength; nor is there any difference in this respect when strengthening the energies that form the human soul.

Whoever cannot in the midst of his everyday, without reclusion and world-rejecting mannerisms, serve the growth of his soul, will certainly not cause his soul to grow; not even if he made company with tigers and snakes in Indian jungles, or had himself immured for the rest of his life in a Tibetan monastery.

If I were permitted by the primal source that gave my timeless spiritual consciousness its life, I could fill volumes with accounts of my experiences in spheres perceived in life beyond, concerning the condition of such jungle hermits and ascetics after they had left their earthly forms behind them.

That much, however, I am free to say: not one of these unfortunates had ever, at the time of his transition, already reached the goal he thought he had attained on earth, given that his body's subtler fluidic energies had credibly deluded him in this belief.

In the midst of life in the world, wherever one might have been placed, one needs to serve the growth of one's soul.

Seclusion may at times prove beneficial, whenever one begins to feels the sensitivity for the perception of the true soul's energies to be in danger of decreasing; but any such seclusion should be only brief, and merely serve to reawaken that perceptive sensitivity. As soon as that is done, one should return again to one's accustomed daily life.

There are only very few human beings on earth whom permanent seclusion does not harm; but despite their separation, even these exceptions live in close connection with their equals; nor would they live secluded lives if they did not have duties to perform that of necessity require an external state that could not be maintained amidst the turmoil of material life.

They only live in solitude as workers in a *Temple* that must remain protected from all the unrest of the world; and they remain in this seclusion solely while their work requires it, not by any means as weaklings "fleeing life."

Nor does one further the growth of the soul by painstaking research in books, by philosophical insights, or by searching for the hidden forces of nature.

All these things one is able to do, having long since relinquished one's soul.

A peasant plowing his field, or a coolie carrying loads, may attain the highest growth of the soul, no less than the most learned mind among the leaders in science; but none will achieve that goal who fails to perform the demands of his station in life, in the mistaken belief that one may better advance the growth of one's soul by leaving the world, or one's class and profession.

"WHOEVER SEEKS to preserve his soul shall lose it; and whoever will lose it shall bring it to life."

This cryptic saying means to point out, among other things, that "leaving the world" in order to find the soul can never achieve that aim; instead, that the growth of the soul can only be found where least expected—in active life in the midst of the world.

Only through active conduct in everyday life can we further the growth of our soul. It is not possible to serve only the soul by excluding everyday life.

It is no more than cowardice and indolence, or a misled philosophy, if one imagines that a life exclusively devoted to the growth of the soul, and removed from the world, could ever achieve what human beings on this earth are able to attain only through the constant struggle with the energies of the world.

One doubtless may further the body's mortal, subtler, fluidic energies by fleeing from life in the world, but no one shall ever advance the growth of his soul who will not daily test its powers anew, in facing the resistance offered him by "the outside world," and the aims of the many around him.

THUS, IN HIS earthly life, also the Lord of Love would often go up "into the mountain," or seek seclusion in order to "pray."

And so he taught, "When you pray, go into your room and close the door."

But he never taught that one should flee from the tasks of the everyday, nor did he himself ever timidly avoid the bustling life of his time and of his people.

He ate and drank what others ate and drank, and he celebrated with them at their festivals.

He was a guest of "sinners and publicans," no less than of those who deemed themselves the purest in piety. He "sat at meat" with learned scribes, but also with the former "woman of many sins."

Wherever he is, the "kingdom of heaven" is near him, because it abides in himself.

He lives the wisdom that he teaches his pupils, showing them how the soul for its growth needs action in life.

છ૭

CHAPTER FIVE

SPIRITUAL GUIDANCE

PAST COUNTING ARE THOSE WHO IN THESE days are searching for spiritual guidance; and among them again are vast numbers who believe they have found, and are following, "spiritual" guidance, while in fact they are influenced merely by impulses originating in the wide-ranging sphere of mediumistic manifestation.

There once again is need "to distinguish among spirits."

Not every voice that one is able to discern within is the voice of a spiritual guide, the voice of divine direction.

More widespread than most people would suspect there is today a variant of mediumistic manifestations that make it all too easy for the lemurian denizens in the invisible part of the material world to satisfy their craving for attention in the consciousness of human beings by abusing their victims' ability to write; and this they accomplish either by suspending the latter's cerebral control, or by usurping their brains' functions and use.

In general, every human being can become a spiritualistic "medium," even though the degrees of mediumistic potential occur in very great variety.

Nor does it matter in the least in this respect whether someone deliberately seeks to become a "medium," or regards himself superior to all the phenomena that are part of so-called Spiritualism.

Whoever trusts an "inner voice" that wants him to be passive—which thus would influence him to obey its utterances, to regard them as suggested guidance, indeed as inner mandate—puts himself in danger of becoming a dependent thrall, a "medium" of those lemurian parasites. In any case, he is already such if his hand starts writing "automatically," whatever the content of the message might be. These entities between the spheres, which mock their victims' efforts to "control" them, will present themselves in every instance according to their subjects' understanding of the world.

Pious Christians will believe such guidance comes from "saints" and "angels," indeed from "Jesus Christ," or even "God the Father." The followers of modern day "Theosophy" will feel sublime "mahatmas" are their guides; and others again will be misled to think that what reveals itself to them is their own "higher self," their timeless spiritual essence, flowing forth from the primordial source of God.

As a typical curiosity I here would like to mention that in a number of cases, as I was told by those involved, the lemurian boundary creatures thought it was effective to make their victims believe their "spiritual guide" was "Bô Yin Râ." As can be seen, one may be granted honors completely unawares.

In one such case the people involved had never heard my name and only learned about my books through what they took to be their "spiritual" guidance. At first they were reluctant to ask about them in a book shop. Yet when they found there actually existed an author by that name, they naturally felt thoroughly convinced that it was I whose guidance they received.

The commentaries to my writings I was later shown, supposedly transmitted by myself during the spiritual session with the medium, were in fact not bad at all, but obviously remained entirely within the conceptual horizon of the automatic writers.

In another case I even was bombarded with rather insulting letters when I tried to rectify the error caused in the séance. Indeed, one did not hesitate quite seriously to make the amusing claim that I was not even the "real" Bô Yin Râ: "the venerable Master" whom one knew to be one's guide, and who had written my books. Part of this claim, to be sure, contained more than a grain of truth.

Such follies can people, who elsewhere are clearly not lacking in critical judgment, be led to commit when influenced by their "spirits."

NAIVELY TRUSTING spiritualists have thus come up with the intriguing explanation that among their "spirits" there may indeed be quite deceptive, as well as droll and playful natures, but that one likewise will finds others, full of kindness, love, and dignity in nature.

As criteria of distinction one innocently accepts the "revelations" provided by the "spirits" themselves; and if such utterances happen to warn of evil things and recommend what is good, then it seems proven beyond any doubt to honest believers that the "spirits" they deal with are "good."

If only these things were as simple as they appear to be in certain minds!

Perhaps that "science," which in these circles is reviled, would not so foolishly reject the spiritualist hypothesis, but long since had with flying colors deserted to the camp of Spiritualism.

Instead, even a researcher of the rank of William Crookes declared, at the conclusion of his successful experiments, that, while he was convinced he often had experimented with invisible intelligences, he could not by any means support the spiritualist hypothesis that these entities were deceased human beings, or their surviving souls.

Surprisingly, however, every thoroughgoing spiritualist even now considers Crookes to be a stellar witness for the cause.

To be sure, one gladly would not touch the creed considered sacred in circles of fanaticized believers in Spiritualism if this dogma did not generate a flood of evil that psychiatrists, and even criminal statistics, can document in sad detail.

One therefore cannot emphasize often enough that the only proof which spiritualist manifestations provide is the fact of the manifestations as such; and that proves merely what also Crookes was right in judging as established fact, namely that invisible entities are able to produce particular effects, by making use of human organs, and thereby can impress the consciousness of mortal human beings.

Beyond that fact, however, nothing else is "proven."

CONCERNING THE nature of these unseen entities one cannot trust experiments to offer any clarity; and it is nothing less than childlike foolishness to assume that the utterances of these beings, transmitted through a medium, and what they say about themselves, are sufficient evidence to draw reliable conclusions pertaining to their nature.

After all, I do not automatically believe a person who calls me on the telephone and claims to be the "emperor of China."

But anyone who knows the sources causing errors, and the potential for deceptions, also clearly recognizes that there are virtually no safeguards against one's being duped in the most brazen fashion by the invisible communicators.

When St. Paul refers to "discerning of spirits" as being a gift of the Spirit of God, he truly speaks of something very different from such unduly credulous receptiveness.

From these invisible lemurian creatures on the border of the physical world you will receive both the loftiest teachings and the most trivial banalities; indeed, even the crudest obscenities, depending in each case on what provides the greatest pleasure to the invisible communicators, which operate without control.

Simply test your venerable "spiritual guides," from whom you only heard high-sounding words of piety, and tell them they are liars if they pretend to be departed human mortals or spiritual teachers; and that you now want nothing more to do with them—and you will be shocked to see the kinds of "friends from the spirit's world" on whom you had bestowed your trust.

There is no lack of former "spiritualists" who came to be cured in the end by rather drastic experiences, and all can confirm what I say.

Still, I understand if you fall prey to deception.

You will receive communications that make it quite conceivable if you believe to be in contact with "departed loved ones"; for to these creatures much is like an open book which to your eyes is hidden under heavy veils; and their uncanny cleverness can easily detect what will convince you most effectively.

To them, nothing is "sacred," and they know neither "good" nor "evil."

They merely are possessed by the desire that you acknowledge them as *actually existing entities*, and want to most effectively impress you; no matter whether they achieve this end through lofty sayings, vulgar insults, through prophesies and wise instructions, through playing pranks, or simply childish folly.

If you believe that in this way you will come into contact with departed loved ones—even doubt may conceal the wish to believe—you shall receive the most attentive service here as well; yet in this case the possibility exists at least that the creatures on the border of the invisible side of the physical world, which are deceiving you, may become transmitters of "messages" from the conceptual realm of those who have died, but whose ascent from low development of spiritual nature has not yet begun.

Yet never will you in this way come into contact with the departed themselves, regardless of the level their spiritual development has reached.

Never!

As long as the earth has borne human beings, invisible entities of the physical world were eager to offer themselves as "spiritual guides" wherever such guidance was sought.

Indeed, human beings let them fulfill even higher ambitions; and many a "miracle" working "god" of ancient and, in certain cultures, even of modern times, is to be found in their ranks, which encompass many different kinds, from levels of mere animal instincts to an intelligence that far surpasses human range.

It is often not surprising that the uninformed will trustingly and full of veneration surrender to such entities' hypnotic influence; for in effect it is no more than that.

The victims disregard the fact, or think it quite in order, that the seemingly so venerable "spiritual" guidance increasingly commands their *will*, and that in subtlety calculated steps it seeks to gain possession of that *will*.

At first one may be given astonishingly good advice, especially pertaining to one's outer life; or possibly predictions that turn out to be correct, and thus are met with even greater awe.

If the victims then appear sufficiently secure in trusting faith, they often will receive "instructions" they should follow.

They will be persuaded to believe they have a special "mission" to perform, or must accomplish one thing or another; and in response to such imagined "spiritual" guidance the most absurd of follies have been carried out.

IN OTHER CASES, where too aggressive action might cause the victim, already well ensnared, still to escape from the influence of the invisible parasites, these will content themselves with playing the part of "enlightened spiritual guides," carefully avoiding whatever might arouse suspicions in the mind of their deluded prey.

The uninformed has no conception of the instinctive cunning with which his trusted "spiritual friends" pursue their aim; nor does he suspect that they know more about his wishes and most secret inclinations than he does himself; and that they shall exploit all things which may seduce him willingly to make himself their prey.

This *willingness*, however, is required if a human being is to fall into the clutches of the unseen entities on the fringe of the physical world; and that requirement at once shows very clearly how any such dependency can safely be avoided.

THOSE WHO SEEK authentic spiritual guidance should first of all grow sure within themselves and recognize that they shall never be approached by any genuine guide from the eternal Spirit's realm as long as they are satisfied with no more than the pseudo guidance which I here had to describe in some detail.

Truly to guide in the Spirit's realm is given only to those here on earth who comprise the circle of Luminaries of primordial Light; and among them only to the one in each case to whom such guidance has been entrusted because his soul's *vibrations* correspond to those of the seeker he is to guide, given that the *rhythm* of their sense perceptions proceeds in parallel patterns.

But such a guide shall never secretly attempt in any manner to subordinate the seeking person's will to his own; nor shall he ever try in any way to eliminate the latter's will.

He shall at all times let the seeker's own will decide whether he chooses to pursue the silent inspiration, or wishes not to do so.

His spiritual guidance, being almost imperceptible, will always allow to partake of his own knowledge; it never will urge that a counsel be followed, although indirectly it offers much useful advice.

But in no case will he ever hypnotically "suggest" that the seeker follow a particular course of action, or conduct himself in a certain way.

Never shall authentic guidance entrust a seeker with a pretended "mission"; never shall it call upon him to perform "great deeds" in outer life; nor shall it ever in the slightest way attempt to influence his temporal existence.

It will also never try to gain a seeker's trust by offering predictions, will not award him any names, nor give advice concerning physical events.

Genuine guidance will always consist exclusively in taking part of the inner life of one who attained perfection in God; and it will accord exactly with the degree of perceptive capacity already achieved by the seeker.

The inner guide will be present with his, as it were, *passive* nature of "speaking" whenever the seeker—by way of his actions—"calls" for his help; and he will be unaware of the guide's presence once he no longer feels that his guidance is needed.

Like a friend, having become one with him in his innermost, he will guide the seeker without revealing himself other than through his own inner life in the Spirit; as an image serving the seeker as a "model"; as the radiant infusion of a spiritual essence, which solely instructs through its very existence, without depending on questions and answers.

THOSE WHO SEEK such genuine spiritual guidance should keep far away from all curiosity about the guide's personal life in the outer world.

The seeker should avoid all questions concerning his own, or the spiritual guide's external conditions of life, let alone those touching other events of the temporal world.

Indeed, even in purely spiritual things he should not ask any "questions," but quietly wait, in calm concentration, until what had as yet remained unclear explain itself, through *insight* granted by partaking in the spiritual teacher's inmost knowledge.

The authentic spiritual guide is fully aware, without being asked, where clarity is still demanded in the seeker; but he also must consider time and circumstances, which offer the conditions under which the seeker is capable of apprehending final clarity within; because the soul is not in every situation, nor at all times, truly able to receive, without distortion, the image that the Spirit's rays can lastingly impress upon its substance.

Again, one surely must not hope for spiritual guidance by a Luminary of primordial Light on earth as long as one remains a captive of the vain conceit that one possesses absolutely certain knowledge, and that the inner guide as well must of necessity subordinate himself to its inexorable logic.

Nor should one assume that one can reach authentic spiritual guidance if one wishes to enjoy it merely as a pastime, on the side, and still is so remote from spiritual reality that one mistakes the Spirit's light for mental acrobatics, and thinks that one can find it without guidance; in effect, intending to deliver the expected guidance to the scrutiny of captious dialectics.

Only "such as are from God do hear God's voice"; and solely the abundance of Light that is in the "Word," which is "with God," and which is "God" is being conveyed when a genuine spiritual guide appears in the life of a soul.

May my words, which are based on experience, and already have helped not a few, also succeed in freeing many others from the grip of the mollusk-like tentacles in which they have ensnared themselves.

May these words assist in showing many who seek, and are mature enough to find, the way to genuine spiritual guidance!

But those who feel their holiest beliefs offended by what I was compelled to say, let them forgive me at present, and, convinced of their honest endeavor, patiently wait for the day when their eyes, too, shall be opened.

It is recorded that also the sublime Master of Nazareth had been tempted several times by the "devil."

Radical fasting had unexpectedly induced a mediumistic situation in the Anointed One.

But he resisted the temptation, and from then on had the power that could "drive out devils," which were nothing other than the lemurian creatures, inhabiting the invisible part of physical nature, of whose presence I am here compelled to warn.

ॐ

CHAPTER SIX

OCCULTISTS' EXERCISES

NOW THAT THE CRUDEST FORM OF philosophical materialism has closed its empty shop, and the natural sciences no longer are regarded as the source of knowledge that alone assures salvation, not a few that in the past had felt they could leave "heaven" in the care of "angels and sparrows," are turning their attention to the problems of the supernatural; and since in their earlier research they acquired a technical method which there had led to success, they automatically assume they can transfer this method, this technique, to the dimension of the supernatural, even though the latter's structure is profoundly different.

But what at best they may achieve this way will make them recognize only too soon that here they operate with tools that prove inadequate.

Now they either abandon their search completely, convinced that where their tools have lost their usefulness nothing of much value can be brought to light, or they continue experimenting, and thus fall prey to the invisible domain of physical nature, which then they regard as the "spiritual" world they are seeking; but since this dimension offers them only sparse and doubtful results, they sooner or later begin to fill in the blanks, by means of speculative thinking, wherever reality has fallen short in delivering facts.

But here we still are dealing with people who should be taken very seriously, while at the same time another type is claiming center stage who in a clever way merely uses the appearance of scientific examination in order to propagate a dizzying hodge-podge of mystagogic flummery, either to gain followers to gratify his own high self-esteem, or for the benefit of some ambitious seeker after fame who did not feel sufficiently appreciated in his earlier work, which still had been of scientific nature in the proper sense.

And now one hastily concocts a "science of the spirit" from everything that one has read in more or less trustworthy literary sources; and this mysterious elixir nourishes all those who did not wholly measure up, by purely scientific standards, in spite of doctorate and honors, but here now see a field before their eyes in which one may, by following the celebrated model of the "great teacher," pursue one's aims quite undisturbed by any scientific interference. One thus may without effort become famous as a great "initiate" if one but diligently practices the "exercises" prescribed by the "teacher of deep secrets," of which he has an ample store on hand for everyone who seeks his counsel. "Exercises" picked, with equal nimbleness and lack of conscience, from those of Ignatius of Loyola, but also from the most pernicious tractates of poison mongers East and West.

WHAT HARM IS done if here and there one of the pupils of "secret science" ends up in an asylum; if the hapless ladies of a certain age age, who form the "great teacher's" worshipful circle, become hysterical; or if the all too simple-minded faithful are ruined in body and soul?

"Secret science" is bound to claim its victims; and the revered teacher of its secrets has long since trained his pupils in a way that almost on command they fall upon the wretch who lost his way to put the blame for his ill fate on him alone; for under no condition would one dare to question the "great teacher's" infallible wisdom, as otherwise one might incur the risk of losing one's own enjoyable position as a cardinal of such a newfound pope; indeed, the entire circus pantomime that is performed might thus unwillingly be facing an untimely end.

To avert that fate, a flood of "exercises" is unleashed; and mass psychosis proves infectious much like whooping cough; for there is still no lack of brains with armor-like resistance that can endure all these procedures; and those who truly can sustain them will then be permanently immunized against all arguments of common sense, against all earnest psychological critique of what is happening within them. They can no longer even want whatever their "great teacher" does not will; and being modest, all the latter wants is to see the world at his feet, no matter how that goal might be achieved.

But let us look beyond this farcical buffoonery which, after all, could only have arisen because the time was ready, and our present age is ill, desperately ill, so that in its despair, for which the regular physicians have no longer any real cure, the public blindly rushes after every nostrum sold by quacks.

Instead we here shall quite in general examine what real worth might still potentially be hidden in "occultists' exercises"; for even outside the groups described above there is no shortage of people who expect all sorts of things conceivable and inconceivable from such mysterious practices, and who torment themselves with foolish ceremonies, or psychic feats of acrobatics, because they hope that in this way they might outsmart the cosmic order and learn the craft of magic; at least to become as wise as the serpent in paradise, which reportedly knew how one becomes "like the gods." Its trusting pupils merely failed to eat the celebrated apple "in the proper way," and so the teachings offered did not produce the desired effect.

AND THAT exactly is the problem with those "exercises": one simply must not make any mistakes when performing them, or else they unfortunately produce the opposite of what was intended, and that may not be pleasant.

On that they all agree, the great adepts of magical lore, who, for their part, cannot move a piece of straw in ways other than Tom, Dick, and Harry, but know all the rites, ceremonies, formulas, and exercises that are needed to let every law of the cosmos cheerfully dance to the tune of their pipe.

It would not be difficult to collect an enormous library of writings on "magic," preserved from ancient times and multiplied in modern days; but I would like to be shown even one among the enthusiastic admirers of these writings who actually managed to reach, beyond all skeptical doubt, at least a single result of all those promised to the novice in these texts with mystifying wordiness if he precisely follows the instructions which, according to their authors, had led them to results.

It thus appears that all of these, including not a few of obvious intelligence, who let their minds be clouded by such writings, without achieving anything besides, had merely failed to exercise "correctly."

Yet long ago there had lived one who said, "If you have faith like a grain of mustard seed, you can say to that mountain, 'Move hence to yonder place,' and it shall move; and nothing shall be impossible for you."

And in another passage he is recorded to have said in a similar sense, "If you had faith as a grain of mustard seed, you might say to this mulberry tree, 'Be plucked up by the root, and be planted in the sea,' and it should obey you."

He, too, had his pupils, and they requested of him, "Lord, strengthen our faith!"

And here we finally have reached the core of all authentic magic power, of spiritual wisdom in practical form.

Here, too, there are "exercises," only their essence is entirely different; and all who ever practiced them gained tangible results. Yet these are not "occultists'" exercises, however mysterious their nature might be; and those who perform them have no need of either ceremonies, or rituals; nor of conjurers' incantations, or of bewildering spells. And yet they work *magic*, contained in the *Word*, through which they will reach the *primordial Word*, in whose *Name* they accomplish all things.

But this *Name* is not a word of any particular language one merely needed to pronounce in a mysterious way. It is rather the sublime eternal energy the Master of the Gospels had called *faith*; and the mysterious way to *utter* that *Name* is the art of all arts: the power of making that *Name* one's inner *experience*.

All the "exercises" of this authentic magic art have but the single aim of learning how to experience that faith in oneself; they do not aim to teach occultists' powers, nor seek to train "clairvoyant" seers, or fakirs who perform their tricks.

Admittedly, authentic spiritual exercises are on the one hand easier, but on the other more difficult than those occultists practice, because unlike the latter, which require concentration only for some hours, they instead engage the human being's whole existence; all one's daily actions; everything one does and leaves undone. They want to see a *new* and *different* human being rise from the material that until then had only served to form the mortal creature; and this transformation must leave no impurities.

Everything that until then had furthered the pursuit of life must now forgo itself that henceforth it may live through *faith*.

ONE THOROUGHLY misunderstands the concept *faith* if one assumes the transformation that is here required, which is to make the human being capable of living in *faith*, is merely a change of opinion; a question of "belief" or "unbelief," as commonly understood, in respect to certain books considered "holy writ"; or had anything to do with the rejection or acceptance of particular claims expounded by religious teachers.

If those attain *eternal life* who "believe,"— who live in *faith*—they surely do not reach that goal because they hold a given doctrine of metaphysics to be true, but because they acquired the capacity of using the energy I here discuss; because they live by the power of *faith*, by the power of the *Name* that is the *Word*, which is "with God," and which "is God."

Correctly understood, "to believe" means to have *faith*, in the same way that "to live" means to have *life*.

A TURNIP LIES before you on the ground. I subject you to hypnosis and compel you through suggestion to "believe" (here *not* in the usual meaning) that you are incapable of picking up that turnip, and you will struggle in vain even to loosen it from the ground.

I release you from your bondage in hypnosis, and you can lift the turnip with great ease; indeed, you would laugh at anyone who doubted your ability to do so; for now you no longer merely "believe" (here in the usual meaning) in the truth of the statement, "I can lift a turnip from the ground,"—this truth you "believed," in the sense of accepting as fact, also while under hypnosis, despite my suggestion to the contrary; for otherwise you would not even have made any attempt to lift it—but now you *effectively* "believe," which is to say, you feel the energy within yourself to lift the turnip from the ground; and this same energy, by means of which you can in fact at any time pick up the turnip, is nothing other than the *faith* demanded by the Master of the Gospels.

Needless to say, it ought to be employed for more important matters than the hapless turnip used here to exhaustion.

This *faith* is not the certainty, acquired through experience, that one is able to perform a certain act, but the *energy* by means of which one can in fact perform it.

There is a subtle irony in the double meaning of the word the Master of Nazareth addressed to the doubting Thomas, "Because you have seen, Thomas, you have believed" (have accepted what you heard as being true) "blessed are they that do not see" (have not gained certainty through experience) "and yet do believe."

A striking play with the word "believe," in which the Master employs it first in its everyday sense, but then alludes to the teachings he had been presenting for years.

Whether or not "historical," this saying nonetheless suggests more clearly than many other things the sovereign style in which the Master used to teach; how he sought to sharpen the minds of his followers, nor always refrained from word play and irony.

Yet this is not by any means the only saying of this kind; and more than one of similar nature has later given rise to furious dogmatic controversies.

YET WHAT IS the connection of the energy that in his teachings he called *faith*—for valid reasons, despite all risks of misinterpretation—to that which through "occultists' exercises" is meant to be achieved?

Here one first of all must clearly recognize that there are two profoundly different kinds of energies that earthly senses are unable to perceive, each determined by the realm of life within the whole of universal Being of which they are a part.

Both kinds are—each in its domain—the *ultimate reality* that underlies all its phenomena; and either represents, in its respective sphere, a lower level than the phenomena they manifest.

When saying that these energies, in their respective spheres of action, *underlie* all manifested worlds experienced as phenomena—and there are physical as well as spiritual orders of such worlds—this should be understood as if I were to say that colors *underlie*, engender, every work of painting, regardless of the subject it presents; in other words, that the material of the colors is the painting's *ultimate reality*, although what is presented through the colors reveals an infinitely more significant reality, but one whereof I here am able to be conscious only by virtue of the colors' substance.

Likewise, however, our consciousness perceives all of the physical universe only because the hidden energies of physical nature *underlie* all of its forms—as their ultimate reality—and because we, being a part of this nature, while living in physical bodies, are equally one of these hidden energies, and thus possess, in our seemingly so coarse material bodies, the *instrument* of its fluidic, subtler energies, which most people mistake for their "soul"; but other animals possess this *instrument* as well, even if in widely differing degrees of effectiveness.

Yet even as the entire physical cosmos manifests itself as purely the effect of hidden *physical* energies, so also are the spiritual worlds made manifest as purely the effect of hidden, objectively existing, *spiritual* energies. Considered as such, however, the latter energies are nothing other than the ocean-like realm of the *soul*, which lies between the world made manifest through physical perception and the domain that spiritual senses manifest.

Just as in the physical world we are able to perceive, to be "conscious," only because we are ourselves one of that world's hidden physical energies, and thus possess in our bodies the subtler fluidic energies of that world, so also are we able to perceive spiritual reality, to be conscious in the Spirit's world, only because we are, at the same time, one of the latter's hidden spiritual energies, and thus possess within ourselves a hidden spiritual organism—an organism purely of the soul— lacking which we never could perceive the Spirit's worlds, nor ever consciously exist within the Spirit, because the soul's dynamic energies are the sustaining *substance* of these worlds.

Now if one practices "occultists' exercises" in the real sense, including what in India is known as Hatha Yoga, and many other things that also in the West have been pursued since ancient times, one merely uses the subtler fluidic energies of the material body; one thus engages exclusively the hidden physical energies of nature; and owing to inexorable laws of physical reality, one in this way becomes entrapped by, and subservient to, the entities that have their spheres of action in earthly nature's invisible realm; one unfailingly becomes "possessed"—having forfeited, as the popular saying goes, one's soul to the "devil" —for the actual soul, the hidden spiritual organism, suffers damage in proportion to the degree that the subtle fluidic energies of the body are delivered to those creatures, which have no sense of good or evil and are beyond accountability and morals.

There will proceed a decrease, a gradual dissolving, of the timeless soul's dynamic energies, which should have formed an individuated, everlasting organism, as whose servants the body's subtler, fluidic energies were to have been employed.

One truly can attain astonishing capacities by means of Hatha Yoga, or similar "exercises," which not the least involve a certain training of breath control in connection with fasting, sexual abstinence, vegetarian diet and the like

—but in this way one never will get closer to the Spirit's worlds. Indeed, one thereby locks, by one's own efforts, the very portal leading to the realm whose radiant substance is the Spirit; and no might on earth is able to open it again in mortal life.

ONE MAY consider it a blessing that that these "exercises" are, luckily, not quite so easy to perform as all the sorcerer's apprentices assume, and that the most effective methods of this kind, while they are known to some Orientals, at least are nearly unknown in the Western parts of the planet.

Not a few who thus would gain "occultists' powers" are playing a dangerous game; only despite all their efforts they fortunately are not going about it "the right way"; and also those who merely pass such "exercises" on to others have no more than some vague ideas, while, for the good of mankind, that which is essential remains to them unknown.

But even in cases of accidental success, which may at times occur, the pitiable practitioner of such "exercises" has gained nothing more than the ability to perform, mostly to the detri-

ment of others, various occultists' tricks—
with the help of creatures that, could he see
them as they truly are, would fill him with horror; or he may succumb to the wildest delu-
sions these entities produce in his mind.

It is a kind of *active* "spiritualism," if one were
to call the activity of "spiritualists" involving
a "medium" the *passive* sort of the practice.

The end of those who once have entered that
path is never pleasant, and in most cases far
worse than even that of a "medium."

This subject I sufficiently discussed in other
books.

In sharpest contrast, both to the methods and
also the results of such practices in the sphere
of the hidden energies of physical nature, proceeds the employment of the magical energies
of the Spirit, the engagement of the soul's dynamic energies to accomplish works of truly
magical nature.

Already in Heliodorus we find, in the third
book of his *Ethiopica*, a novel highly regarded
also as a literary work, the following passage,
revealing wisdom and knowledge:

"The one kind of magic is for the common herd and always crawls, as it were, low on the ground; it consorts with ghosts and burdens itself with corpses; the other kind, however, for whose attainment we priests and prophets struggle all our lives from early youth, is looking toward heaven, keeps company with the gods, and partakes of the nature of powerful beings."

Who could here still have any doubt which kind of magic the Master of Nazareth had taught to his pupils?

And the instructions he gives to attain this genuine magic lead the pupil higher step by step.

Reading the Sermon on the Mount, one will see which general "preliminary exercises" he considered absolute requirements; seeking "exercises" for the more advanced, one will find that each of his parables speaks volumes; quite apart from his unmistakable words to his chosen pupils:

"To you it is given to know the mysteries of the kingdom of heaven; the others are told of it only through parables."

In the parables he emphasizes the only thing required in all "exercises": the readiness of our consciousness to apprehend the stirrings of the soul, and our will's resolve to follow what the soul's dynamic energies demand.

But to his chosen pupils he also showed the practical effectiveness of spiritual laws.

To them he disclosed why it was necessary to act according to the parables' advice.

To them he also revealed how one drives out "evil spirits"; namely those borderline creatures of the invisible part of the physical world, when they cause harm to the soul.

In this way he introduced his pupils, at times comprehended, at other times misunderstood by his listeners, to many teachings of wisdom that can be "revealed" to the "little ones and babes," but remains "hidden" from the conceited "prudent and wise."

But even so he said, "I have yet many things to say to you, but you cannot bear them now," and thereby advises his pupils that within everyone who has been truly prepared "the Spirit of truth," the Spirit's divine scintilla— the *living God*— will appear in the timeless *self* of the soul; and he will "guide them into all truth," will only "take from what is mine," even when he came to speak through the mouth of another.

Mystery surrounds the two-fold meaning of this word; for everything the Anointed One himself had given came from the ocean of spiritual treasures revealed by the *living God*, whom he bore in himself, having become consciously one with His Being, like each of those he called "his own," whom he foresaw as his coming successors.

"If I spoke from myself, I would be a liar; now I do not speak from myself, but what the Father has told me I say unto you."

None of those who speak from the Truth conveys *from himself* what he teaches; and no one has authority to show the path to union with the Spirit who does not bear the Father live within him—who does not live in consciousness united wholly with his *living God*.

THERE IS NO need that here I once again repeat the guidelines I already have provided in many parts and forms in other books.

I was permitted also to say things the Master of Nazareth could in his day not yet disclose to his pupils, his "disciples," because for them it would have been "too hard to bear"; and this I could do only because all of it has long since been made known to the public at large, if in distorted form, without being given attention.

It was necessary to shed light on these topics because the corrupted form in which the world has until now been told about them has already caused immeasurable harm, and such damage was at last to be contained.

It therefore is important to make it clearly understood that only those are sometimes able to enter the hidden world of physical nature without peril who possess the needed faculty from birth, and then were schooled by a guide having authority securely to master the forces at work in this realm.

The only guides in this, however, are the *Luminaries of primordial Light*, the "Masters" of the "White Lodge," who had to become sovereign rulers of the hidden energies of physical nature before in this temporal life they were entrusted with the key that alone can open the portal through which all human beings on earth can enter the path that leads to the realm of the Spirit.

One who in this way has rightfully gained the ability to employ the subtler fluidic energies of the body may also in a given case employ them beneficially.

To all others, however, these energies are bound to cause their undoing.

By contrast, what all without exception will develop for their benefit and blessings are the hidden *spiritual* energies at work in the realm of the soul.

How one learns to use these energies, safely led by inner guidance, which reaches all who on their own will honestly and with resolve begin to exercise these energies *through action*, is described in great detail in the teachings I have given form; and these are drawn from no source other than the wellspring of timeless wisdom the Master of Nazareth had called the "Spirit of Truth," which he knew to be forever inexhaustible, bestowing blessings even on most distant generations.

$$\approx$$

CHAPTER SEVEN

MEDIUMISM AND ARTISTIC CREATION

FOR THOSE WHO WITNESS THE MANIFESTATIONS a medium produces it seems to be extremely difficult entirely to disregard the nature of the product which the unseen entities involved are able to bring forth.

If one receives communications sounding noble and sublime, or even suggestions for the everyday, which may in fact prove useful, one instantly is ready to ascribe the contact to "higher spiritual guidance"; and this belief at times may go so far that people blindly will entrust their earthly fate and fortune to the influence of beings supposedly from "higher realms of Spirit."

Participants are not aware of being in a state resembling hypnosis, and therefore willingly obey the impulse of a will controlled by someone else.

What the beings here in question are in fact, however, I have described in detail in *The Book on Life Beyond*, in *The Book on the Royal Art*, and also in the present pages. We here are dealing neither with "departed loved ones," nor with higher or lower "spiritual beings," but with invisible entities of a part of physical nature normally barred to us.

These beings are neither "good" nor "evil," nor are they bound by moral laws. Their sole desire is to manifest themselves to human beings; and certain individuals with the needed psycho-physical disposition serve them as suitable instruments for purely their own satisfaction.

Subject to cosmic order, these beings are active as form-producing agents within the realm of physical perception.

And so it should not be surprising that also in their deviant attempt to manifest themselves where they are, as one might say, out of bounds, their actions will result in generating forms.

THERE IS A wide range of manifestations of these beings in which, according to their nature, they express themselves as form-producing agents; among them is likewise their use of a medium to generate semblances of drawings and paintings, a phenomenon frequently observed in the history of mediumistic practice.

I have personally witnessed enough such manifestations, and observed far more astounding examples of that kind; only with the difference that I had firm control over the beings that were using the medium, so that they were forced to do whatever I wanted.

Especially the manifestations in the field of painting appear, at first glance, to be rather harmless; but this is not at all the case.

Every contact with the beings here involved demands of the medium a complete, or nearly complete, surrender of the impulses of its own will. The medium thus delivers its energies into the hands of those beings, which, lacking all sense of responsibility, seek merely their own gratification, no matter whether the soul of the medium will thereby be injured, or not.

These beings always seek, and instinctively find, the weakest point in their victims' inner resistance.

They lure each prey with the bait it will swallow.

The influence of these beings on the energies forming the soul is comparable to the destructive effects of viruses and other microbes on the health of the physical body.

One therefore cannot recognize the danger promptly enough, however "beautiful," "awe-inspiring," or "interesting" the phenomena might appear.

Even if no damage is observed at the moment, it never fails to leave its mark; and in most cases where the danger is not dealt with in time, the harm incurred will be irreparable.

One cannot warn enough against all playing with such entities, which are entirely removed from one's control.

DURING THE creative process, every genuine artist doubtless serves his inner god; and certainly he knows the "inner voice," and how to "hear within."

And surely he, too, cannot tell whence the spirit descends that imbues him.

But when and where did any creative artist ever have to surrender himself to that spirit as a medium does—feeling its hand mechanically moved, seeing works taking shape that were not the result of personal talent and craftsmanship?

Where is the creative artist, from Dante to Goethe, from Giotto to our most recent modern painters who did not have to labor for the form that would give its truest expression to what moved him within? Who did not have to study for years to gain the foundation on which alone he then could become a servant of his god?

Never shall the artist's *inspiration* deprive him of the power to control his will. Never shall it turn him into a mechanical device. In fact, the contrary takes place.

All painstakingly acquired skills are summoned; every inner faculty the creative self possesses gains consciousness and life to a heightened degree; all the energies that form the soul feel light and free, while the artist's *own self* holds sway in ways so immensely powerful that the artist later, once again part of everyday life, appears to himself as a stranger, inclined to believe he could not be the same person that, during the hours of creative work, was able so masterly to bring all of his soul's potential to light.

Where is here anything vaguely resembling the passive state of the medium, which is made to move much like the frog's legs through which Galvani observed the effect of electrical current? A tool that hardly needs to look at the work for which it lends its hand, while its own self is not in the least engaged in the entire operation, because the entity that is in fact at work can far more thoroughly exploit his victim if it heeds him as little as possible, ideally in a state of trance, when its consciousness is relinquished completely.

BESIDES, WHATEVER these beings produce through their mediums is never anything original; for while, according to their nature, they lend to matter form, they are not able to create a form that is original; they are incapable of having their own thoughts, nor do they have their own ideas in the domain of forms. Consequently, where they do not serve, according to their proper station, the impulses of cosmic will, but seek to control a medium, they have to glean and gather their material from images and concepts that had been formed by human minds.

Occasionally, their reproduction of such mental images remains unchanged, so that one easily can trace the source from which they stole what they present.

More commonly, however, they weave their presentations from a random lot of scrambled fragments, whether in the field mental "revelations," or as paintings and drawings produced by a medium.

It here is necessary clearly to distinguish between truly artistic creation, and a medium's passive activity; as otherwise we risk a vicious confusion of concepts.

As I am thoroughly familiar with the subject discussed above, I was obliged to present the truth; the more so since this variant of lemurian possession as well is all too often venerated as a sign of "heavenly grace"; while in this book we carefully seek to differentiate between things that are by nature forever incompatible.

❧

CHAPTER EIGHT

AT THE
WELLSPRING
OF LIFE

ASSUREDLY, THERE IS NEED TO SPEAK OF timeless Truth in ever new and different images—the Truth one cannot apprehend except through parables and symbols, because it is Reality, primordial Essence of all Being, the very wellspring of all Life.

Nothing in our days prevents the confusion of minds.

Every testimony of inner experience is brought to light from moldy crypts, from dusty shelves of libraries, and offered to the trembling hands of seekers like pronouncements of some oracle.

From all directions do seekers accept whatever there is, and what can be found. Sleepless nights they restlessly pore over voluminous tomes; in every pocket they carry with them the most questionable tractates as if they were holy writ; with reverence they listen everywhere to the cryptic utterances of teachers devoid of authority; and in this way believe they might yet, in the end, discover the path that leads to the wellspring of Life.

The heads are crammed with the most ludicrous fantasies of enterprising mystagogues; a strange variety of "science," probing things that never yield to "scientific," study, presents itself with lofty gestures in word and print to an astonished world; the arsenals of human superstition of all ages are scoured and left empty; spook of the weirdest kind is once again in vogue.

Yet all this confusion is only created by the desperate longing of hearts that are starving; and many who run with airs of elation after the latest country fair prophet had merely come because they would not miss at any price what could perhaps give clear direction to their aimless search.

THE VICTIMS who fall prey to such unconscionable clutter-brains and brazen prattlers are not by any means the most uncritical of seekers.

Not a few, however, who let themselves be hoodwinked wake up in time to see the light; and then they recognize with shame and indignation that the "guidance" they had trusted did itself not know the way, nor even where to find it; indeed, that they had followed "guides" who never truly cared to guide them, but merely had with cunning minds espied the weakness of their fellowmen, and dangled bait before those longing to find knowledge, to lure them into their own nets.

Also among the readers of these words are likely to be quite a few that in this way have been profoundly disappointed.

And yet, despite their disappointment they still may sense there must exist a path on which they truly could attain the goal they long to reach.

To all of them is here especially addressed what follows.

THOSE WHO are determined, despite all past mistaken ways, not to abandon their quest till they have found their soul's desire, will truly find the path that leads them from entrapment out into the open, the narrow path that leads to living Light.

Many times I have already shown that path, and do so here again for all who want to find it.

There is need for guidance on this path because it leads through many a trackless jungle in which the unsuspecting wanderer encounters tempting by-ways of great danger; it also leads through deserts, in which the trace of every step is covered at once by the sand, so that the path must be prepared for everyone anew.

It thus would be not only foolish, but presumptuous if those who seek were to assume that here they could distinguish the authentic path by trusting their own judgment.

It would no less be foolish and presumptuous if boldly they felt capable to reach their highest goal without first having passed the tests that try their strength, which they must meet at every new stage of their path.

Finally, it would be foolish and presumptuous if they believed that they could in themselves attain their highest goal—*conscious oneness* with the primordial wellspring of all Being—without the help of those who long since have achieved that goal.

They would be like a climber who sought to scale the highest summit of a mountain range directly, in a beeline from the plane, without first having mastered the approaching crests surrounding the central peak, the heights from which alone the right path can be shown him to the range's highest summit and to the goal he longs to reach.

To THE UNCRITICAL listener it may sound very brave if someone demands that "nothing must stand between himself and God." However, the "God" such a believer imagines he can feel, is a deceptive God; a construct purely of the mind, and therefore no more real than any other mental fiction.

The "God" such pious dreamers worship may doubtless for a while give comfort to believers bound to him by faith; he well may awaken energies in them which even strengthen the illusion that here they encounter the primordial wellspring of all Life. Within eternally immutable Reality, however, such a "God" is no more than a phantom, incapable of affecting even the least of the events objectively existing in absolute Reality.

Those who feel content with such a pseudo experience of "God" are even less likely to find their *living God* in themselves than may the so-called "atheists," who in most cases deny the existence of God only because, in one way or another, they have generally seen through the pious illusion, which the others embrace, who think they converse with "God," on a first name basis, but in truth worship solely a phantom of thought.

The "atheist" is doubtless in the right when he denies that such a "God" exists; his error is only that, having recognized the phantom as a phantom, he fails to make the effort to search for the reality that lies behind the fiction.

He at least may one day still encounter the objective experience of *God*—who is Life in Himself—while the believer, in bondage to his self-created pseudo "God" can seldom free himself again from the chains he has forged by his mind.

Yᴇᴛ ᴛʜᴇʀᴇ are also other forms of self-deception, and many seekers have already fallen in such traps.

One of the most important, which plays a problematic role in the lives of the majority of "mystics," will here be discussed in particular.

Wɪᴛʜᴏᴜᴛ ᴀɴʏ kind of inner guidance, nor any help from those who have awakened in the Spirit, every human being is able to perceive a spiritual light within, appearing as the image of a flaming star, for which the monks of Mount Athos felt such veneration that in their view no other name would worthily describe it but "the sacred light of Godhead."

Not only the monks of the Athos monasteries, but also many other mystics and seekers after God allowed themselves to be misled, in that they took this light as confirmation that their soul had come to be united with the *living God*.

In reality, however, they merely had experienced a faint reflection of their own lives' highest form; and so they worshiped their own selves, convinced they had encountered God.

What they beheld within themselves was no more than that essence of their spirit's life, which only can awaken in timeless radiance when the *living God*, in fullness of power and truth, will makes it the throne of His glory; when, in the *human being on earth*, He will come to be "born as the child of the virgin"; proclaimed by "shepherds keeping watch at night;" adored by the "wise men from the East," the royal priests of the *innermost East*, who everywhere can see the "star," as soon as it shines above a "stable" in which, "amidst animals lacking discernment," the king is born who will bring "deliverance" to Israel.

Many have spoken in ecstasy of their "re-birth"; of the intimate "friendship" of their soul with "God"; of the spiritual "marriage" with the "heavenly bridegroom"; many believed the task was accomplished and "nirvana" attained, yet merely had perceived the inner image of the *flaming star*, which first must be empowered eternally to shine; but that power solely the *primordial Word* is able to bestow; nor can anyone attain it who will not take the path that the *primordial Word* itself is compelled to prepare for the Spirit's fallen progeny, that it may once more come within that power's reach.

As human beings we do not live our lives in isolation. We all are but the issue of eternally creative power, and are as such connected with each other by a thousand secret threads.

Whatever goals are to be reached, never can one individual succeed without another, and all great goals of human effort are realized by the harmonious interaction between one human life and others.

If we insist, at any cost, to accomplish something by ourselves alone, without the help of others, we thereby merely demonstrate that we still do not understand ourselves as being what in truth we simply are, and likewise have been, from eternity, before our "Fall."

We then are bound to go astray, even if with purest heart and will we were to seek the loftiest of aims.

Nor can human beings ever attain their highest goal, the experience of union with their *living God*, in fullness of Power and Being, if they believe they are able to do so without the guidance that eternal wisdom and mercy has provided for them out of compassion.

Human beings are in need of such guidance; for thus it is founded in cosmic existence as such; nor will it diminish their worth in the least if they ask for assistance; even as the other, whose task it is to offer help, does not thereby increases his worth, given that he, too, had once required help, before he grew able to bring it to others.

Here each hand will always pass on to another what it, too, had received; and none possesses out of himself what then he can give to the next.

It is from the radiance of the *primordial Word* alone that the "word of the Lord goes out to the ends of the earth," preparing for each age the *Luminaries* here on earth, who then are able to bring light into the darkness of their fellow humans, whose eyes have not yet opened; given that after the "Fall," the human being who has not been prepared—long before his mother gave him life on earth—is not able, without help, to apprehend the Light that radiates from the *primordial Word* alone; the Light that can let only those become transformed into the *Word* who had accepted, of their own free will, millennia before the earth would offer them concealment in a creature body, a burden that is hard to shoulder for a mortal; a yoke that very seldom finds a human who succumbed to the "Fall" and yet will in the end elect to bear it, moved by mercy and compassion for humankind on earth.

Only those who thus have been prepared to be the *Word* are then entitled to instruct their fellow humans in matters that pertain to final things; and mankind has throughout the ages received such firmly rooted guidance, through teachers' words whose fundament was God.

Not a single human being born and nourished on this earth in all the ages has at any time attained his highest goal, the conscious union with the *living God*, without the spiritual help of those whom the *primordial Word* appointed to be helpers.

They alone ought to be trusted; and whether a teacher is in truth of their kind, the voice of the heart will never leave any doubt; unless it is drowned by the noise of deceptive teachings, whose bondage one had uncritically made one's prison.

Authority is here not proved by wondrous feats, and no authentic helper of his fellow humans will ever stoop to boast of fakir powers.

While it is possible that he may master forces which people as a rule regard as "superhuman" and "miraculous," such "signs and wonders" even then are merely secondary side effects of his activity and, like other gifts of similar nature, purely the result of the special capacity of his psycho-physical organism; but faculties of that kind can never give proof that he has been appointed.

The seal of one who truly has authority to offer help will always be found in only the seeker's innermost depth, which no plummet shall fathom, nor mundane opinions and prejudiced thinking can ever invade.

Those who in that inmost realm will weigh their teacher's words, by no self-fashioned notions' lure misled, nor yoked to other minds' opinions, will never be deceived by teachers without calling.

They shall be led to the wellspring of Life, to that sublime *primordial Light* which knows itself as the *primordial Word*, and utters its

Words, throughout the aeons, as living individuations in the Spirit's realm.

In the way a poet, from words of human language, composes epics, lyrics, and hymns, even so the *primordial Word* composes from its *Words*, and by it own creative power, its eternal hymn of glory, in form of endless hierarchies of spiritual individuations; and the final echo of these hierarchies is heard in the Brothers of the "White Lodge," which from time immemorial has sought to bring Light to the earth; for its members alone have the Spirit's authority to bear witness of life in the Spirit, which they objectively know from timeless experience.

Thus proceed, from the *Word* that is *God*, from the self-articulation of eternity's *primordial Light*, all the rays that ever sought to kindle Light on earth.

Only those will find this passing comprehension, or open to doubt, whose inner life is still devoid of insight into the sublime reality, exceeding all descriptive powers, which, in its highest sublimation, discerns itself as *God*.

ONE NEEDS TO have some knowledge of the ranks of this eternal Life, and of the forms in which it is unfolding, if one seeks profounder understanding of the mystery *God* truly is, and how the real *living God*, in infinite self-generation of His Being, wrests Himself from His own essence to generate eternally new aspects of His Being.

One needs to recognize the difference between the One who reigns above all heights and depths, as He encompasses all things within existence, and the "God" that human thought, alas, construed, in often more than strange configurations.

There are some who have declared that "Everything is God," and "In every atom of this world of physical perception ought you to discover God!" Or similarly, "All external aspects of this world are but illusion, and all things are in truth not "things," but "God."

This may be said indeed; and if one seeks to grasp its sense correctly, one may regard it as a truth; even though this truth courts highly questionable understanding.

If one intends to find the human spirit in oneself, however, such playing with mere words will hardly bear much fruit.

If we seek highest knowledge of the truth, we must let things continue to be "things," even though they may not ultimately be what they appear; nor must we deify them even in the subtlest sense.

We otherwise incur the risk of paying godlike honors to a manifested form of timeless Life —from which the Godhead without ceasing creates itself anew—merely because it passes human comprehension; and at this level we may bind ourselves so thoroughly that it becomes impossible for us ever to encounter the reality of *Godhead* in its majestic radiance.

THIS ETERNAL Life, which constitutes the Godhead's timeless "sustenance," forever manifests itself in threefold form, in each according to its own dimension, as the universe of physical nature, the oceanic realm of the soul, and the kingdom of the Spirit.

No "creator" has brought any of these realms into "existence."

All is but the manifested form through which the *one* eternal Life reveals its Being, which, although itself supreme above these three domains of manifested forms, within its highest conscious essence crystallizes its own Self as the *primordial Light,* as the quintessence of what human beings can in truth experience in themselves, by adoration overwhelmed, as the primordial wellspring of all Life—the human being's *living God.*

WHILE BEING the cause of its Self in all its manifested forms, this *one* eternal Life yet reaches the fulfillment of its highest Being only beyond all manifested forms; even though each of its manifested forms is likewise of its essence, but serves it purely, figuratively speaking, as the "ocean of renewal," out of which, by its own self-effected power, it forever generates itself anew.

It thus was said, "To be his sustenance has Brahma formed this world"; only here one must not be misled by exoteric concepts and think of a producer and his product; because this saying of the Vedas conveys far more to the informed. To them it reveals Reality's profoundest depth; it unveils the inherent law of

Brahma's self-regeneration; the nature of the one and absolute Existence, being Life eternal of Itself, which thus provides its highest, all-encompassing conception of Itself as *Godhead*, with sustenance in Its three manifested forms.

THE PRIMORDIALLY creative, innate energies that manifest eternal Life in forms of all-comprising physical reality, here then reveal themselves in bringing forth—and in destroying—forms, in order that new forms may be created.

Worlds come into being, and worlds return to dust again, continuously throughout cosmic space; but never was there a "beginning" of cosmic existence as such, nor will there ever be an "end" of that which in itself is Life; which, as Life, reveals its Being as creative power, encompassing within itself the forming and dissolving of all the worlds throughout the aeons.

Even as in this visible manifestation of eternal Life, there are centers of energy that neither microscope, nor any other scientific instrument, however precise, is able to display to human comprehension, so are there likewise invisible owners of highest intelligence in this dimension, whose faculties surpass the powers of the mightiest of human thinkers, much as the reasoning potential of a native in the jungle is exceeded by the intellect of philosophers like Kant or Spinoza.

At the same time, however, this manifested form of timeless Life also contains invisible beings that barely have the intelligence of animals serving humans as beasts of burden.

YET NONE OF these invisible entities are *spiritual* in nature; nor are they even in their highest forms by any means *immortal*; even though their individual lives may extend to thousands of years.

For the highest of these entities, in many ancient cultures they were revered as "gods," nature holds no "mysteries" of any kind.

Everything encompassing the physically manifested form of timeless Life—both its visible and its unseen dimension—is disclosed to them, who are by nature purely intellect, and they have knowledge of its smallest part.

But all that lies beyond this physically manifested form of timeless Life—the whole immeasurable ocean of the soul and the infinite realm of the Spirit— to them does simply not exist.

They recognize no "Godhead," and only feel contempt for human beings' efforts, of which they are aware, to "prove" that "God exists"; because they know that in the sphere of intellect there truly is no God.

They are the source that causes all the over-rating of human mental powers, of all extreme proliferation of the intellect in humankind.

In the physical manifestation of eternal Life, even eternal Life apprehends itself only as all-comprehending *physical* nature, without in itself being conscious of its higher manifestations, whose forms are the realms of the soul and the Spirit.

SHARPLY DIVIDED from its manifestation as all-comprehending physical nature, set apart from it by an unbridgeable chasm of sense perception and feelings, yet even so pervading this initial manifestation, the ocean-like realm of the soul reveals its infinite wealth of sense-conscious forces and beings.

All of these are *conscious* both of the existence of all-comprehending physical nature, but likewise of the Spirit's world; meaning they are able clearly to experience the effects they apprehend from either realm.

Likewise sharply set apart, both from the ocean-like realm of the soul, as from the world of physical nature, although pervading either manifestation of eternal Life, there is the time-less kingdom of Spirit with its innumerable hierarchies of self-aware, self-apprehending, thinking, sentient, and through direct percep-tion knowledgeable, everlasting spiritual Be-ings, whose individuations endure beyond decay—the highest form in which eternal Life's infinities can be experienced.

In a sequence of infinite levels, one rank of perfection rises above another, until, to draw upon an image, the apex of that cone of Light shines forth in fullest radiance. Conscious of its own eternal life, in highest knowledge of its Self embracing all its Being—its conscious-ness awakened in *primordial Light*—it lives that *Light*'s own essence, therein becoming the *primordial Word*, the self-articulation of absolute eternal Being, which once again en-genders life in all three manifested forms eter-nal Life comprises.

Here we have reached the wellspring of Life; the fountain whose waters eternally pour from its depth, and which forever causes all things it had sent forth at last to return to their source.

I KNOW FULL WELL that human language proves inadequate, and unavoidably becomes mere stammer, if it attempts to describe what can be apprehended only in the Spirit, and purely by direct perception; yet even so I think that some who read these words may feel as if a distant recollection dawned in them, which in their innermost may stir a joyful echo that will direct them to the path that leads the human spirit to its highest goal—the path I seek to show in many forms—more lucidly than if I had kept silent.

To be sure, everything is here described merely in images; however, one should bear in mind that most of it entirely eludes the grasp of language, so that necessity would keep it secret, even if I meant to write a heavy tome on every word here touched upon. Out of profoundest veneration for the ineffably sublime reality that is the subject here presented, I have intentionally avoided also the traditional terminology that human thought has coined in its attempt to apprehend eternal things by mental speculation.

I THINK I offered what the title of this chapter promised; yet only those will benefit from what it teaches who on their own set out to search for the wellspring of Life, and will not rest until they have discerned its trace within themselves; even if its *living water* can reach them only through the channels that it has itself created, so that human spirits on this earth, despite their *Fall,* may still receive it, making them desire more, so that, after aeons, they shall one day know the blessings of eternal Life in all its fullness through the ages without end.

He that gave his life at Golgotha, and in his death had caused Love's highest might to flow again, from depths of primal Being, into life of physical existence, has cleared the path that leads to the wellspring of Life, for the sake of all who truly seek to follow him.

What he had once accomplished, for all humankind, those alone are capable of comprehending who already have entered upon the path to their own liberation, and thus can feel the power that the work of Compassion's greatest Mediator allows them to receive on the path they have elected.

Such will also comprehend the meaning of the radiant Master's word,

"And I, being lifted up from the earth, shall draw everything to me."

They alone will likewise be able to use the *magnetic* power—drawing back to *primordial Being*—which that exalted Luminary once had wrested from its chains by his all bounds surpassing Love.

❧

CHAPTER NINE

MEMBERSHIP IN "THE WHITE LODGE"

DESPITE THE FACT THAT I IN MANY places have repeatedly and very clearly written about the work and nature of the spiritual community of which I am a member, and spiritually obligated, without choice, to make its teachings public, I time and again am faced with the question, "under what conditions" one could gain admittance to that community, referred to as the "White Lodge"?

Strangely, some of the inquirers even make bold to report that someone had told them he had been admitted by me.

In truth, I can hardly understand that even one of the persons concerned could have made such an error.

Be that as it may, however, let the following immutable statement once and for all serve them for their orientation: I never could admit any person, whoever it be, into the spiritual community referred to as the "White Lodge"; that I, consequently, never could have told anyone, whoever it be, that I had "admitted" him to the "White Lodge"; and that I never can recommend any person as a candidate for admittance.

Such a statement appears to be necessary, even though I truly left no doubt that during life on earth no human being ever could be "admitted" to the "White Lodge"; given that each of its members is already born as such, after in his spiritual existence, millennia before his earthly human birth, he had accepted the commitments that exclusively determine who will be a member of this spiritual circle.

ONE SHOULD expect that all of this ought not to be too difficult to comprehend for anyone concerned at all with spiritual matters.

Above all, one ought to be able to presuppose a somewhat more clarified understanding in respect to the changes in one's spiritual dimension of life, which the "admittance" to the

"White Lodge" would have surely brought about, if it could indeed occur in mortal life.

Does one really believe such an "admittance" —assuming it were possible—would have no more profound effects than membership in some religious faith?

Anyone who ever read what I have written surely ought to know that there is mention of the most diverse of spiritual energies which the authentic members of that circle call their own; of their most varied spiritual faculties; and, above all, of the continuous spiritual communication among its members.

The simplest kind of logical thinking should therefore suggest even to those caught in this curious error that they ought to have grown conscious of these things within themselves if they had in fact gained membership in the "White Lodge."

What this displays is an incredibly naïve idea of the real nature of spiritual life. One obviously mistakes authentic spiritual perception —the *reality* of which is felt more forcefully by far than even the most compact form of physical experience—with sundry fancies of imagination; with a kind of wakeful dreaming;

with hallucinations or the effects of influences from the spiritualist domain. One thus seems wholly unaware that any human being who is capable of living consciously in the objectively existing worlds within the Spirit partakes of a completely different form of life, compared to which all things that common usage means by "spiritual" life appear as cloudy shadows, pallid, artificial, and unreal.

Unable to experience its reality, one cannot even visualize the nature of spiritual life; however, after the objective descriptions I provide in so many contexts of my writings, one ought at least to some extent have understood, also intellectually, that here we stand before the highest aspect of Reality that one is able ever to experience.

THE INQUIRIES concerning the conditions for admittance to the "White Lodge," and the offer to found "chapters," further shows that people who already are familiar with various "occult" traditions seem to think that here they came upon a temporal society, dedicated to the furtherance of mysticism, or things of the occult, in the style of the former orders of Illuminati, or the lodges of Freemasonry.

What doubtless has contributed to this impression is the designation "White Lodge," a name that, as one knows, did not originate with me, but which I nonetheless retained, because I felt the dignity attributed by many to that name should obviously prevent the mentioned errors.

On the whole, indeed, events confirmed that retaining the term proved necessary, as otherwise it could have led to the confusing idea that there existed, in addition to the spiritual community from whose midst I speak, a different spiritual society which called itself the "White Lodge."

But in order to remove even the last possibility of making any error, let the following be stated, once and for all, in unembellished words.

The spiritual community of which I am a member and bear witness, is an objectively existing *spiritual* unity—a Oneness consisting of many spiritual individuations, most of whom have either never borne an earthly body, or long since have returned it to the earth. In every age, however, a few of them have also lived and worked in mortal human bodies on this earth but in their outer lives were not in any way distinguished from their fellow human beings, nor in the least exempt from the effects of nature's laws.

Respecting the state of the inner life, however, there is a fundamental difference.

Our fellow human mortals are able to perceive no more than the external physical world, and the life of the soul's dynamic energies; but the spiritual worlds' reality they can at best divine; to our consciousness, however, the Spirit's realm of radiant substance is fully accessible, even to the highest levels that a simultaneous existence in an earthly body still permits.

We consciously experience, at the same time, the external physical world, the dimension of the soul's dynamic energies, and the Spirit's realm of absolute reality, without needing any preparation other than directing our focus toward any of these worlds.

WE DO NOT behold the Spirit's worlds in states of ecstasy, nor any other abnormal conditions, but fully awake, in lucid sobriety; and no external signs of any kind would let the casual observer suspect that our consciousness is not, at a particular moment, exclusively directed toward the physical, external world.

Furthermore, we are in permanent conscious spiritual connection among ourselves, as if a constant electrical current were continuously flowing through us all, including those who are not physically embodied.

Whether or not we meet each other in our physical bodies is not of importance.

When we meet in this way, the external encounter thus only involves the temporal person.

By means of spiritually given reality we can make ourselves seen and heard among each other simply by an act of will.

Although on earth we have what might be called a "center," where some of us at all times live in absolute seclusion from the outside world, we conduct no external "assemblies," made quite unnecessary besides, owing to our constant spiritual connectedness.

We also for that reason do not observe any kind of external ritual, nor perform any manner of ceremony.

We know who belongs to us, without need of external signs.

No one can be one of us who has not already, as stated earlier, belonged to us even before he was born on earth in a mortal body.

"Membership" is nothing other than the consequence of a commitment, voluntarily accepted, millennia before the member's birth.

This commitment is accepted in a spiritual state which, to the present consciousness of human beings, is now inaccessible, even though each mortal born on earth had once passed through its stages.

Also the members of our spiritual community have knowledge of that distant former state of their existence only through their purely spiritual individuation, by virtue of unmediated memory.

The physical organism and the soul's potential of such a human being must first be rendered capable, in gradual stages, guided by those who have reached their perfection, so that the spiritual energies and capacities may be transmitted to that person's sphere of conscious will; but that schooling proceeds from within, even if the *Brother* who will guide this unfolding is physically present, visible in his temporal body.

The members of this spiritual circle living on earth are not "saints," nor are they shielded from human shortcomings.

AGAIN, WE ARE not "fakirs" of some sort; that is to say, we never under any circumstances stoop to deal with any practices of the "occult," with "magical ceremonies," or matters of that nature; even though the possibilities in question are fully known to us and we would be at any time quite certain of success.

In our work we exclusively engage the energies of the objectively existing *spiritual worlds*; in other words, we initiate, according to inexorably binding spiritual laws, the respective spiritual causes, of which the consequences in the worlds of the soul and of physical nature, result in beneficial transformations affecting humankind.

In this we act by no means purely according to our personal judgment, but under the direction of higher spiritual orders, which in turn reflect precisely given conditions that only seldom can be altered by our wishes.

As can be seen, one obviously is here not dealing with a circle of "adepts," a more or less religiously colored "secret society," a school of "occult science," nor for that matter any kind of corporation held together by external constitutions and decrees.

Although such temporal associations had at times entrusted themselves to the guidance of this purely spiritual community, none of its members has ever belonged to any such external society in his outer life, except as its spiritual mentor.

ONE CONSEQUENTLY never must assume that any external secret society mentioned in historical records, however mysterious in appearance, was in fact the "White Lodge."

We here are dealing with something so fundamentally different, so utterly singular and concealed from the world that all attempts to search for traces in outer human social life can only lead to error and confusion.

The only thing a carefully examining observer may at times detect in human history is the result effected by the beneficial spiritual influence of that community within the Spirit, whose Oneness unites many members.

Finally, in order to dispel even the last remaining source of error, let it be expressly stated that members of this spiritual community had not seldom offered guidance to the world through spoken words and writing, but that before it had been made my spiritual obligation, these things have at no time been spoken or written about in language all can understand, such as now is done by me; and more than merely one millennium will pass before one of my future Brothers in the Spirit will be able to continue the work I began.

That also this external work is founded on the universal plan of spiritual activity of which the "White Lodge" is a part, will need no special explanation for discerning minds.

Nonetheless, for all I am obliged to say, I certainly do not deny that more by far must even now remain a secret, and shall continue to be such forever; given it can be entrusted only to those on earth who, by their own volition, had undergone a trial of their powers, lasting for thousands of years. before they could receive a human being's mortal garb, born of a mother's body.

I hope these explanations will suffice at last to silence the question of how one becomes a "member" of the "White Lodge," and that in addition they will also clarify some other points, which many readers may find helpful.

THE TEACHINGS I transmit contain their truth within themselves, but they cannot reveal their deepest roots except to those who want to experience that truth in their own inner lives. May this book, too, become a way to inner experience for many!

Not until it has become experience—not until its teachings are lifted above the domain of theoretical considerations, in order to imbue one's everyday life, can it open its reader's eyes for the liberation from the night of unknowing.

Knowledge about teachings that lead to timeless life can bring forth liberation only if those informed will turn such teachings into practice by their deeds.

He that, as a true and real *high priest*, once had drawn the timeless mystery of blessings down upon all beings on this earth—he that, in his death at Golgotha, had accomplished the all-surpassing deed of Love—what else had been his will but that his teachings would find practical expression in active life on earth?

If this book is to explain to you the mystery of Love, which he, whose Love exceeded every measure, had once brought into being, in his death on earth, all my words will be of little help as long as you shall not yourself attempt to experience their truth in your own life and actions.

From the selfsame wellspring flowed his teachings, as do the words that I convey.

If you are determined to find what here can be discovered, you must be willing to devote your whole existence to the quest of a reality that only those are able to discern who seek to find it, in simplicity, and free of all conceit of mind, within themselves, and in their own experience.

But then shall truth forever become your shelter.

You then shall know what it means: *consciously to live eternal life.*

Then you will yourself bear witness to eternal truth.

☙

CHAPTER TEN

FOLLIES OF IMAGINATION

FAITHFUL TO MY SPIRITUAL BEING'S ORIGIN, I here am bound explicitly to warn again a literary genre presenting sundry "world views," which nowadays demands increasingly more space on book store shelves, and casts its fascinating spell on ever larger groups of seekers, but whose offerings, examined by light, reveal themselves in every case as merely yet another curious compilation of underripened fruits of reading.

Some of the originators of such literary products belong to the peculiar human species of the self-elected, who cannot rifle through five books without thus feeling qualified and called upon to write a sixth book on related matters on their own.

Others again have actually read nearly everything that human hands have written down throughout the ages to offer answers to the questions plaguing human hearts and minds, who long for a reality beyond a world in which the fear of suffering and death looms like a dreaded specter behind all forms of joy.

Encyclopedic reading then is often found combined with well-schooled speculative thought, and equally remarkable ability to put thoughts into words; but the writer in such cases may no longer be aware that pouring out his heart in writing is simply a way of ridding his mind of a burden; and so his brain will risk the strangest leaps, only that his head at last may clear itself of the accumulated heaps of fallen fruit picked up in reading, and by habit stored in memory, which he had gleaned from every field of thought, from every pasture of religious creed.

Even truly venerable knowledge in the strictest sense of sober-minded science will not by any means protect against the same kind of compulsive self-appeasement, which, all too free of doubt, goes hand in hand with the conviction that actual reality "must" necessarily be structured according to its mentally elaborated model.

Reality, however, is altogether independent of the conceptual images and mental constructs mortal brains create, and whose reflections humans use to shape their inner worlds.

The wealth of earthly knowledge, which thinking can amass, and concepts may illuminate, should not mislead one to assume that, consequently, the results of mental effort, and of explanations, provide effective instruments to modify reality.

Immutable, consistent purely with its own inherent laws, reality mocks all designs to change its given structure; nor can any human mental power alter what is truly real; yet very little wisdom proves sufficient to indulge the follies of imagination that make the human mortal think he can control reality according to his whim.

The sort of literature to which I here refer consists without exceptions of such follies of imagination.

Relatively harmless are such books and pamphlets if their foolishness is so apparent that even those not yet informed and warned can readily detect it

Far more damage will such writings cause, however, if the mind of a fanatic, skilled in logically persuasive forms of exposition, presents in them a mixture of his brain-spawned jelly with sundry fragments that reflect authentic aspects of reality.

Every time the reader encounters such a fragment in the slippery mass, he touches something firm and solid; he then feels sure that some objective truth must correspond to that specific feature of the presentation; yet then he carelessly draws the conclusions that, therefore, all of the gelatinous concoction truthfully bears witness to reality.

What follows next is that the reader fears he might deprive himself of finding truth if he were critically to probe things on his own; but once such fear gains hold of him, it finally will paralyze his independent judgment, which still could have enabled the cleverly baited victim to free himself from the hook.

There are substantial numbers of highly respectable men and women who, as earnest seekers after truth, originally had hoped to find believable reflections of reality, but then had lost their freedom, as described above, for the rest of their lives on earth.

The waste of national wealth committed by nearly all the "civilized" countries of the world, in order by such methods to bewilder peoples' minds and fill their hearts with fear, may in this context be mentioned only in passing.

None of the authors of the literary genre to which I here refer appears to consider whether he is able to accept responsibility, also after his physical death, for that which in his days on earth he teaches with a voice so thoroughly persuasive, and may perhaps regard as justifiable in his own mind.

Nor will many lose much sleep over such a question since in their heart of hearts they subscribe to the notion that after the death of the physical body all further experience is bound to cease anyhow.

But even where the author has become imprisoned by the hodgepodge of conceptual worlds that he invented, nothing seems to be farther from his mind than the faintest inkling of doubt as to his right to proclaim his constructions.

Regrettably lacking in such cases is awareness of responsibility; and it pains me deeply to be forced to say that even works of singular poetic talent will not in the least offset the poisonous effects to which the organism of the soul is unavoidably subjected wherever people speak on final things without authority and calling, as if this were a topic to be molded according to one's taste and mood.

At most, it may be understandable if a shepherd of souls in the service of a faith, who depends on its given store of images and concepts, continues to teach as he was taught he had to teach, even though his insight long since has outgrown such teachings—but hardly can an unconstrained creative writer, who serves exclusively his art, expect to be judged with the same understanding—and forgiveness—if he makes use of sacred beliefs, and of words that mankind reveres as coming from God, merely to serve the needs of the day, when that day, estranged from veneration, calls for effective ornaments that would deceptively conceal its dreary varnish.

Mankind of the present age is certainly not yet "degenerate," notwithstanding that professional complainers like to claim it is.

Even the prevailing inability of nations to inspire respect for each other, except by instilling fear of horrible weapons of total destruction, displays *ineptitude* rather than actual degeneration.

Humankind is not yet able to grasp the significance of its mechanical conquests during the last hundred, let alone the last fifty years.

As a result, it still cannot in truth possess the conquests it has made, but at this time appears instead to be itself possessed by what it has discovered.

Once that possessive spell is overcome, there also will develop the ability to recognize the deeply-rooted spiritual lessons that wait to be discovered behind the wealth of technical inventions made in modern times.

But even today could open minds take home the obvious lesson from the domain of technical conquests that merely knowing the rules contained in manuals of mechanics is clearly not sufficient, also in this field, to encompass the reality that must be understood before the engineer can make his calculations to begin his work, if success is to reward his efforts.

Only if he carefully adapts his concepts to reality, whose laws no influence can alter, will the machines he has designed be useful for their purpose.

SIMILARLY, EVERY construct of unduly stirred imagination will prove completely worthless when those realities are to be represented which are by nature inaccessible to our mortal body's creature senses, in the only form that these are understood and used today.

Here, too, a person first must have objective knowledge of reality before he can be certain that what his words convey will not cause souls to perish in thickets of intractable confusion.

Among the millions of human beings of all races, however, there are at any time no more than a small number of men who are sufficiently prepared at birth to let reality reveal itself to them, and make them able to endure its essence.

The saying of the ancients, "Whoever sees the face of God must die," has its profound validity for every human being; and even the hand-ful of the truly prepared must bow to its truth, albeit in attenuated form.

No more, of course, than any other mortal am I the origin of these realities; I merely can bear witness of their nature, because I consciously exist within their midst.

The fact that human minds are able to "imagine" all these things in very different ways can never in the least deflect reality from being, and remaining, what it is; nor from exclusively conforming to its own inherent laws.

ALTHOUGH I here am bound to warn against teachers lacking authority, I can only hope, speaking from human compassion, that none of them even vaguely suspects what in his mind he allows his thoughts to treat as a toy.

Objective awareness of the consequences, not to be extinguished in thousands of years, would doubtless prevent even the most unconscionable of literary adventurers from promoting the imagined follies of his mind as true reflections of reality.

In myths and ancient tales, in legends and some teachings of the great historical religions this reality can still be found in truthful images, although today it is so darkened by the soot of countless votive candles that great care and patient effort need to be devoted if one intends to discern at least its fading traces.

Even so, there still is much that here waits for discovery by those whose skillful hands will once again make visible what scarcely can be recognized today; because the founders of the ancient sacred cults had known "that those who see the face of God must die"; and so they had created the images symbolic of reality, as guiding signs for all who hoped to find their *living God* within their *inmost self*, where then His presence is not "seen," but can be felt in every atom of the soul, in every cell of the body, bestowing blessings, power, and illumination.

ALSO LOVE'S most radiant vessel, the conqueror of Golgotha, had "seen" God face to face; for he was one who, at his time, had been prepared; and knowing that he could not make his people aware of ultimate reality, which he discerned and knew, except through images reflecting truth, he taught almost exclusively in parables and symbols.

At times, however, he even sought to reach beyond what parables and symbols could convey, by saying things his pupils scarcely had expected he would tell them.

"This is a hard saying, who can hear it?"

For them it truly had been a "hard saying" when the Master taught with mathematical precision:

"The kingdom of heaven is in you!"

That was not the way they had imagined.

Nor did they find it any easier to comprehend him when he said:

"I and my Father are One. Who sees me, sees also the Father who sent me."

But: "The Father is greater than I."

Such sayings come almost alarmingly close to reality, so that they surely must have seemed quite problematical to those of "little faith," who could of course not yet imagine how subtly Christian scholars, versed in the "knowledge of God," would one day be able to interpret words of that nature.

Today, therefore, one must intentionally pay no regard to such interpretations if the meaning of the actual sayings is truly to be understood.

Far more important, however, than making it one's goal correctly to interpret what has survived until this day of the authentic sayings of the radiant Master, is the *change of orientation* of one's entire earthly life toward seeking "the kingdom of heaven within us."

Even if no other word of Love's most radiant vessel had come down to our time, this reminder alone would suffice to reveal that all human beings are able to find the eternal kingdom of heaven only within themselves— and all according to their individual ability and powers to experience its reality.

And here the uncontrolled ambition to "interpret" ought respectfully to stand aside.

At issue here is *the kingdom of heaven*—the realm of the worlds of the eternal Spirit's radiant substance—not simply a pious feeling of having found imagined favor in the eyes of "God."

And only within ourselves are the heavens open to us that one day shall be our home for all eternity.

In our own self is the portal to all the domains in the Spirit, since our own spiritual self is imbued by them all.

Yet even within your self will you gain admittance to only the "heaven" that accords with your capacity of being conscious in the Spirit; and that capacity can secure its stamp and rank by virtue purely of an active life in the environment that you have made your own.

Once the day has come when you shall lose your mortal body's service, you will have to content yourself with entering the "heaven" that corresponds to what you did to your own self and to your fellow human beings; and ages that exceed all human comprehension need to pass before you can become transformed in ways that make you capable of apprehending also higher realms in the dimension of the Spirit's radiant substance.

Not to yourself alone should you devote your strength, your energy, and care throughout your life on earth, but likewise not exclusively to others.

Here, too, you must be mindful of inexorable laws.

The more closely you are able to approach the harmony demanded by the Spirit's law, the greater wealth you gain in treasures that endure.

May you succeed in balancing also your spiritual "debits" and "credits," even as a prudent merchant makes it his goal in the world of temporal values, then surely you never will have to regret the deeds of your days here on earth.

∝

REMINDER

"Yet here I must point out again that if one would derive the fullest benefit from studying the books I wrote to show the way into the Spirit, one has to read them in the original; even if this should require learning German.

"Translations can at best provide assistance in helping readers gradually perceive, even through the spirit of a different language, what I convey with the resources of my mother tongue."

From "Answers to Everyone" (1933), *Gleanings*. Bern: Kobersche Verlagsbuchhandlung, 1990

Other Works by Bô Yin Râ
published in English translation:

Bô Yin Râ:
An Introduction to His Works

Contents: Preface. About My Books. Concerning My Name. In My Own Behalf. Essential Distinction. Résumé. Comments on the Cycle <Hortus Conclusus> and the Related Works. Brief Biography of Bô Yin Râ. The Works of Bô Yin Râ.

The Kober Press, 2004, 117 pages, paperback. ISBN 0-915034-10-7

This book presents a summary of the essential features that set the author's works on final things apart from the innumerable publications, old and new, that seek to answer questions which thinking minds have asked in every generation. Traditionally, such answers draw upon beliefs, accepted faith, and speculative thought, culminating in systems of religion and philosophy. Rarely have solutions rested on objective insights into the dynamic structure of reality, embracing both its physical and spiritual dimensions. But in addition to providing such direct descriptions of these aspects of reality, the author's books are helpful guides that let the readers gradually develop their inherent faculties so that they may experience this reality themselves. For readers having sensed the nature of this ultimate experience the concepts "spirit," "soul," "eternal life," and "God" are then no longer merely abstract notions based on hope and faith, but have become realities that form the human being's timeless essence, even as they underlie all aspects of creation.

In the first chapter of this *Introduction* the author discusses the origin and purpose of his books; how they should be used; for whom they are intended, and what their application may accomplish. Here he also stresses that his writings neither are opposed to, nor written to support, any particular religious creed, even though the followers of all persuasions may benefit from what they have to offer to all who seek to know.

The following chapter sheds light on the author's name and explains why his books are published under this spiritual proper name, which is not an arbitrary pseudonym, invented for the purpose of effective self-illumination, but expresses, in phonetic equivalents, the essence of his nature.

In the final chapter he corrects a number of misunderstandings of his books and person, typically prompted by hasty judgments, hearsay, or prejudice. Here he also touches on the common source of all authentic spiritual disclosures and stresses that objective insights into that dimension ought to be distinguished from the subjective mystical visions found in the different forms of religion.

The Book on the Royal Art

Contents: PART ONE: The Light from Himavat and the Words of the Masters. 1. The Luminary's Self-Disclosure to the Seeking Soul. 2. The Harvest. 3. The One whose Being is Infinity. 4. Know Thyself. 5. On the Masters of the Spirit's World. 6. Pitfalls of Vanity. PART TWO: From the Lands of the Luminaries. 1. The Threshold. 2. The King's Question. 3. The Pillar in the Mountains. 4. The Night of Easter. 5 Communion. PART THREE: The Will to Joy. 1. To All who Strive Toward Timeless Light. 2. The Teachings on Joy. Epilogue.

The Kober Press, 2006. 198 pages, paperback. ISBN 0-915034-13-1

This work is the first volume of *The Gated Garden*, a cycle of thirty-two books in which the author shows the way that lets his readers find objective spiritual truth within the light that darkness cannot conquer. In this opening volume the author discloses his own spiritual origin and sources and explains the reason leading to the publication of these books in our time. As the Western mediator of the oldest roots of ancient Eastern wisdom he also gives his readers the criteria to distinguish spurious echoes of that wisdom.

Of particular significance for Western readers is the chapter "The Night of Easter," which recalls the actual events preceding what would later be accepted as the Resurrection. In this context the book also touches on the Eastern wellspring in the teachings of the historical Master of Nazareth.

The concept "Royal Art" in the book's title refers to the Indian Raja Yoga, but here the term is used to denote a spiritual craft that far transcends the practices that are today suggested by that name.

As the portal to *The Gated Garden* this book is of particular importance in that is sets the tone and outlines the perspective from which all other volumes in the cycle should be viewed and understood.

The Book on the Living God

Contents: Word of Guidance. "The Tabernacle of God is with Men." The "Mahatmas" of Theosophy. Meta-Physical Experiences. The Inner Journey. The En-Sof. On Seeking God. On Leading an Active Life. On "Holy Men" and "Sinners." The Hidden Side of Nature. The Secret Temple. Karma. War and Peace. The Unity among Religions. The Will to Find Eternal Light. Mankind's Higher Faculties of Knowing. On Death. On the Spirit's Radiant Substance. The Path toward Perfection. On Everlasting Life. The Spirit's Light Dwells in the East. Faith, Talismans, and Images of God. The Inner Force in Words. A Call from Himavat. Giving Thanks. Epilogue.

The Kober Press, 1991. 333 pages, paperback. ISBN 0-915034-03-4

This work is the central volume of the author's *The Gated Garden*, a cycle of thirty-two books that let the reader gain a clear conception of the structure, laws, and nature of eternal life, and its reflections here on earth. The present work sheds light on the profound distinction between the various ideas and images of "God" that human faith has molded through the ages —as objects for external worship—and the eternal *spiritual reality*, which human souls are able to experience, even in this present life. How readers may attain this highest of all earthly goals; what they must do, and what avoid; and how their mortal life can be transformed into an integrated part of their eternal being, are topics fully treated in these pages.

What sets this author's works on spiritual life apart from other writings on the subject is their objective clarity, which rests upon direct perception of eternal life and its effects on human life on earth. Such perception is only possible, as he points out, if the observer's *spiritual* senses are as thoroughly developed to perceive realities of timeless life, as earthly senses need to be in order to experience *physical* existence. Given that authentic insights gathered in this way have always been extremely rare, they rank among the most important writings of their time, conveying knowledge of enduring worth that otherwise would not become accessible

The Book on Life Beyond

Contents: Introduction. The Art of Dying. The Temple of Eternity and the World of Spirit. The Only Absolute Reality. What Should One Do?

The Kober Press, 2002. 161 pages, paperback. ISBN 0-915034-11-5.

This book explains why life "beyond" is not so much a different and wholly other life, but rather the continuation of the self-same life we live on earth. The difference between the two dimensions lies chiefly in the organs of perception through which the same reality of life is individually experienced. On earth we know that life through our mortal senses, in life beyond it is perceived through spiritual faculties, which typically awaken after death. At that transition, the human consciousness, which usually is unprepared for the event, is at a loss and finds itself confused by the beliefs and concepts of its former mortal life. As a result, the new arrival faces certain dangers; for, owing to these mental prejudices, the person is unable to distinguish between perceptions of objective truth and the alluring phantom "heavens" generated by misguided faith on earth.

To help perceptive readers form correct and realistic expectations, that they may one day reach the other shore with confidence and without fear, this book provides trustworthy guidance into spiritual life, its all-pervading structure, laws, and inner nature. Given the unbreakable connection between our actions here on earth and their effects on life beyond, the book advises how this present life may best prepare the reader for the life that is to come.

The Book on Human Nature

Contents: Introduction. The Mystery Enshrouding Male and Female. The Path of the Female. The Path of the Male. Marriage. Children. The Human Being of the Age to Come. Epilogue. A Final Word.

The Kober Press, 2000, 168 pages, paperback, ISBN 0-915034-07-7

Together with *The Book on the Living God* and *The Book on Life Beyond*, *The Book on Human Nature* forms a trilogy containing guidelines toward a new and more objective understanding of both physical and spiritual realities, and of the human being's origin and place within these two dimensions of creation.

The Book on Human Nature at the outset shows the need to draw a clear distinction between the timeless spiritual component present in each mortal human, and the material creature body in which the spiritual essence is embodied during mortal life. The former, indestructible and timeless, owing to its being born of spiritual substance, represents the truly human element in what is known as mortal man. The latter, physical, contingent, and subject to decay and death, is no more than the temporary instrument the spiritual being uses to express itself in physical existence. Given that the spiritual and animal components within human nature manifest inherently discordant aspects of reality, they typically contend for domination of the total individual. Experience shows that in this conflict the animal component with its ruthless drives and instincts clearly proves the stronger.

To help the reader gain a realistic understanding of the human being's spiritual and physical beginnings, by way of concepts more in keeping with humanity's advances in every discipline of natural science, the book explains, to the extent that metaphysical events can be conveyed through language, the timeless origin and source of every human's spiritual descent. It likewise shows that the material organism, now considered mankind's primal ancestor, existed long before it was to serve the spiritual individuation as its earthly tool. In this context the author points out that the traditional creation story, such as it has survived, is not simply an archaic myth, invented at a time that lacked the benefits of modern knowledge, but instead preserves, in lucid images and symbols, a truthful view of actual events. Events, however, that did not happen merely once, at the beginning of creation, but are a process that continues even now, and will recur until this planet can no longer nurture human life.

Even so, the principal intention of the present work, as well as of the author's other expositions of reality, is not so much to offer readers a new, reliable cosmology, but rather to encourage them to rediscover and awaken the spiritual nature in themselves, and thus to live their present and their future life as fully conscious, truly human beings.

The Book on Happiness

The Kober Press, 1994. 127 pages, paperback. ISBN 0-915034-04-2.

Sages and philosophers in every age and culture have speculated on the nature, roots, and attributes of happiness, and many theories have sought to analyze this enigmatic subject. In modern times, psychology has joined the search for concrete answers with its own investigations, which frequently arrive at findings that support established views. Still, the real essence of true happiness remains an unsolved riddle.

In contrast to traditional approaches, associating happiness with physical events, the present book points to the spiritual source from which all human happiness derives, both in life on earth and in the life to come. Without awareness of this nonmaterial fundament, one's understanding of true happiness is bound to be deficient.

The author shows that real happiness is neither owing to blind chance, nor a capricious gift of luck, but rather the creation of determined human will. It is an inner state that must be fostered day by day; for real happiness, as it is here defined, is "the contentment that creative human will enjoys in its creation." How that state may be created and sustained, in every aspect of this life, the reader can discover in this book.

The Path to God

Contents: Fantasy and Faith. Knowing Certainty. Dreaming Souls. Truth and Reality. Yes and No. The Decisive Battle. Individual Perfection.

The Kober Press, 2008. 129 pages, paperback. ISBN 978-0-915034-15-8

While the author's *Book on the Living God* provides a comprehensive overview and introduction to spiritual realities affecting human life on earth and, in the chapter "The Inner Journey," describes the path that leads the human soul to the experience of life's final mystery, the present work outlines a number of essential aspects that readers need to bear in mind as they pursue that path.

As it is of critical importance that the reader's mental concepts correspond, as far as human language permits, with facts of spiritual reality, the book draws clear distinctions between the powers of authentic faith in something that in fact exists, and the innumerable phantoms human minds invented and imposed as objects of belief.

Likewise, in the spiritual domain the concept "knowledge" does not signify the mere accumulation of countless random facts, but rather the ability to comprehend the object to be known by virtue of becoming one with its reality.

The chapter "The Decisive Battle" sheds light on the mysterious entity whom Jesus defined as the "prince of this world," and refers to the destructive influence of that purely temporal being and its place in the physical cosmos.

The path to God illuminated in the book is not the search for an object of emotional worship, but instead, as summed up in the book's concluding sentence, the journey to each seeker's individual perfection in the Ground of Being.

The Book on Love

Contents: Introduction. The Greatest of Compassion's Mediators. On Love's Primordial Fire. Light of Liberation. On Love's Creative Power.

The Kober Press,. 2005. 148 pages, paperback. ISBN 978-0-915034-12-3

Love, properly understood, is not merely, as the author explains, a human sentiment of varying degrees of intensity, inspired by particular objects and, like all feelings, subject to continuous change. Love is, instead, the highest of creation's elemental powers, giving life to and sustaining all dimensions of reality. The human sentiment called "love" is but a faint reflection of that cosmic force and ought to be distinguished clearly from its distant source.

Earthly love in all its forms is typically aroused by the desire of possession for an object. Celestial love, by contrast, is a spiritual energy that manifests itself beyond and free of all desire, independent of external objects. Human beings can partake of the celestial form of love, which then transforms their temporal existence by virtue of their timeless life, and thus will make them more than simply "sounding brass and tinkling cymbals."

In its initial chapter the book sheds light on the historical facts surrounding the life and teachings of the unprecedented figure of Jesus of Nazareth, who, more perfectly than anyone before or since, embodied love's celestial force in word and deed. Empowered by that highest form of love he found the strength to change this planet's spiritual aura in his final hour and freed all human beings of good will from ancient bondage.

The Book on Solace

Contents: On Grief and Finding Solace. Lessons One Can Learn from Grief. On Follies to Avoid. On the Comforting Virtue of Work. On Solace in Bereavement.

The Kober Press, 1996. 126 pages, paperback. ISBN 0-915034-05-0.

In this book the author shows how sorrow, pain, and grief, although inevitable burdens of this present life, can and ought to be confronted and confined within the narrow borders of necessity. Considered from the spiritual perspective, all suffering experienced on this earth is the inexorable consequence of mankind's having willfully abandoned its given state of harmony within the Spirit, a deed that also ruined the perfection of material nature. Although the sum of grief thus brought upon this planet is immense, human beings needlessly expand and heighten its ferocity by foolishly regarding grief as something noble and refined, if not, indeed, a token of God's "grace."

Understanding pain objectively, as a defect confined to physical existence, which, even in exceptional cases, is but an interlude in every mortal's timeless life, allows the reader to perceive its burdens in a clearer light, and thus more patiently to bear it with resolve.

While suffering, through human fault, remains the tragic fate of physical creation, the highest source of solace, which helps the human soul endure its pain and sorrow, continually sends its comfort from the Spirit's world to all who seek it in themselves. How readers may discover and draw solace from that inner source the present book will show them.

The Book of Dialogues

Contents: Testimony. Knowledge and Reality in Action. Light and Darkness. The Spirit's Might. The Jewel of the Heart. Transformation. The Dialogue on the Innermost East. The Dialogue on the Passing of a Master. The Flower Garden. The Deviant Pupils. Night of Trial. Individuality and Person. The Realm of the Soul. On Finding Oneself. On the Elder Brothers of Mankind. Mystery of Magic.

The Kober Press, 2007. 175 pages, paperback. ISBN 978-0-915034-14-X

This book contains a series of conversations between the author as a pupil and his spiritual mentors, before he was himself accepted as a Master in their circle. It touches on a number of essential topics that help the reader recognize authentic knowledge of objective spiritual truth and the nature of those who, since the dawn of time, have conveyed that truth to humankind as spiritually sanctioned Mediators.

The book is of especial interest for its biographical disclosures, as these not merely shed unprecedented light on the development and schooling of authentic spiritual Mediators, but also on the singular position assigned to the author of the present and the other volumes of The Gated Garden.

As the Western representative and voice of the perennial Eastern source from which all timeless insights into spiritual light and knowledge flow, the author shows the way to those who have been guiding human spirits to eternal light since ages immemorial, long before the rise of temporal religious creeds.

While insights from that highest source have reached humanity in ancient days, time and misinterpretations have shrouded their authentic form, nor have they ever been presented to the public at large as an integrated whole in such detail before.

The Wisdom of St. John

Contents: Introduction. The Master's Image. The Luminary's Mortal Life. The Aftermath. The Missive. The Authentic Doctrine. The Paraclete. Conclusion.

The Kober Press, 1975. 92 pages, clothbound. ISBN 0-915034-01-8.

This exposition of the Fourth Gospel is not a scholarly analysis discussing the perplexing riddles of this ancient text. It is, instead, a nondogmatic reconstruction of the actual events recorded in that work, whose author wanted to present the truth about the Master's life and teachings; for the image propagated by the missionaries of the new religion often was in conflict with the facts. The present book restores the context of essential portions of the unknown author's secret missive, which the first redactors had corrupted, so that its contents would support the other gospels.

Written by a follower of John, the "beloved disciple," its purpose was to disavow the "miracles" the other records had ascribed to the admired teacher. His record also is unique in that it has preserved the substance of some letters by the Master's hand, addressed to that favorite pupil. Those writings are reflected in the great discourses which set this gospel text apart and lend it its distinctive tone.

Given the historic impact of the man presented in this work, an accurate conception of his life and message will not only benefit believers of the faith established in his name, but also may explain to others what his death in fact accomplished for mankind.

The Meaning of this Life

Contents: A Call to the Lost. The Iniquity of the Fathers. The Highest Goal. The "Evil" Individual. Summons from the World of Light. The Benefits of Silence. Truth and Verities. Conclusion.

The Kober Press, 1998, 126 pages, paperback. ISBN 0-915034-06-9.

This book addresses the most common questions people tend to ask at times when circumstances in their daily lives awaken their awareness of the many unsolved riddles that surround the human being here on earth. To be sure, philosophy and teachings of religion have offered answers to such questions through the ages, but as these often draw on speculation, or require blind belief, they can no longer truly satisfy the searching mind of our time.

It is against this background that the present book will guide its readers to a firmer ground of understanding, resting on objective insights and experience. From this solid vantage, readers may survey their own existence and its purpose with assurance.

As this book explains, the key to comprehending the meaning of this present life is, first, the insight that this life is but the consequence of causes in the Spirit's world and, thus, has of itself no meaning other than that fact. And, secondly, the recognition that material life is ultimately meaningless if human beings fail to give it meaning: by virtue of pursuing goals whose blessings shall endure. The nature of the highest goal that mortals can pursue provides the substance also of the present book.

Resurrection

Contents: Preface. Resurrection. The Wisdom of Sages.
Effects of Law and Chance. Wasted Labors. Mardi Gras
of the Occult. Inner Voices. The Magic Effect of Fear.
The Limits of Omnipotence. The New Life. Festive Joy.
The Virtue of Laughter. Self-Conquest. Conclusion.

The Kober Press, 2009. 179 pages, paperback. ISBN
978-0-915034-16-1.

The sacred concept "Resurrection," historically associ-
ated with the Master of Nazareth, who had affirmed "I
am the resurrection and the life," has through the centuries been faithfully misunderstood as the resuscita-
tion of his dead and buried mortal body. The present
book explains that the event of which he spoke was not
a physical but spiritual transformation, which can, and
ought to, be attained by human beings even in this present life. This *spiritual* reawakening is independent of
religious creeds, but solely the result of conscious actions, thoughts, and words

What the "resurrection" of the spiritual consciousness
within the human being's animal nature presupposes is
the foremost subject of all the writings of this author.
Here he discusses in particular some common miscon-
ceptions that prevent or hinder the attainment of this
goal. At the same time he provides the reader with in-
structive guidelines that are helpful on this inner quest.

Worlds of Spirit
A Sequence of Cosmic Perspectives

Contents: Preface. The Ascent. The Return. Reviews of Creation. Epilogue.

Illustrations: *Emanation. In Principio erat Verbum. Lux in Tenebris. Te Deum Laudamus. Space and Time. Primal Generation. Seeds of Future Worlds. Emerging Worlds. Birth of the External Cosmos. Labyrinth. Desire for External Form. Astral Luminescence. Sodom. Inferno. De Profundis. Revelation. Illumination. Fulfillment. Victory. Himavat.*

The Kober Press, 2002. 96 pages, 20 full-color illustrations, hardcover. ISBN 0-915034-09-3.

If all the books of Bô Yin Râ, objectively considered, are unparalleled in the extensive literature on subjects touching final things—in that their author did not publish speculations based on faith or thought, but gave the reader fact-based insights into spiritual reality—the volume *Worlds of Spirit* occupies a special place even among these thirty-two unprecedented works; for in this book he integrated twenty reproductions of his paintings, representing *spiritual perspectives*, to illustrate selected aspects of his text.

While the works of the *Hortus Conclusus* cycle constitute the first authentic, comprehensive exposition of metaphysical realities, the paintings in this volume represent, in turn, the first objective visual renditions of spiritual dimensions in their dynamic figurations, colors, and inherent structure. Together with the written word—the book describes events experienced and perceived by an awakened human spirit—the images are meant to offer readers lucid concepts of nonphysical existence, and thereby to assist them in developing their own perceptive faculties.

On Prayer

Contents; The Mystery of Praying. "Seek, and You Shall Find." "Ask, and You Shall be Given." "Knock, and It Shall Be Opened Unto You." Spiritual Renewal. Let This Be Your Prayer: Twenty-Two Prayers.

The Kober Press, 2010. 138 pages, paperback. ISBN 978-0-915034-17-8.

In this book the author clarifies the fundamental difference between appeals addressed to an imagined God, who lives by only his believers' faith, and thus cannot fulfill their many wishes—and real prayer, which unifies the human spirit's will with the objectively existing wellspring of all Being, whose Mediators offer help and guidance to all who learned the sacred art of praying.

As the book explains, praying is an art one can and needs to learn, so that what is requested may be heard and answered. This learning brings about a transformation of a person's inner life, and leads to heightened spiritual self-awareness.

While there are limits to what prayer can effect in mortal life, it remains an indispensable source of strength and renewal in physical existence. Its highest gift, however, is the help it offers human beings on their way to conscious spiritual life.

Spirit and Form

Contents: The Question. Outer World and Inner Life. At Home and at Work. Forming One's Joy. Forming One's Grief. The Art of Living Mortal Life.

The Kober Press, 2000. 108 pages, paperback. ISBN 0-915034-07-7

The underlying lesson of this book is that all life in the domain of spiritual reality, from the highest to the lowest spheres, reveals itself as lucid order, form, and structure. Spirit, the all-sustaining radiant *substance* of creation, is in itself the final source and pattern of all perfect form throughout its infinite dimensions. Nothing, therefore, can exist within, or find admittance to, the Spirit's inner worlds that is devoid of the perfection, harmony, and structure necessarily prevailing in these spheres.

Given that this present life is meant to serve the human being as an effective preparation for regaining the experience of spiritual reality, this life must needs be lived in ways that are consistent with the principles that govern spiritual reality; in other words, ought to be lived according to the structure, laws, and inner forms of that reality. To show the reader how this present life receives enduring form, which then is able to survive this mortal state, the book sheds light on crucial aspects of this physical existence and advises how these may be formed to serve one's spiritual pursuits.

❧

THE KOBER
PRESS

www.ingramcontent.com/pod-product-compliance
Lightning Source LLC
Chambersburg PA
CBHW022123080426
42734CB00006B/232